THE
COSMOS
FROM
SPACE

Also by David H. Clark

Superstars
The Quest for SS433

THE
COSMOS
FROM
SPACE

David H. Clark

Crown Publishers, Inc.
New York

Published by Crown Publishers, Inc.,
225 Park Avenue South, New York, New York 10003,
and represented in Canada by the Canadian MANDA Group

CROWN is a trademark of Crown Publishers, Inc.
Manufactured in the United States of America

Library of Congress Cataloging-in-Publication Data
Clark, David H.
    The cosmos from space.
    Includes index.
    1. Astronomy—Popular works. 2. Astronomy in
astronautics—Popular works. I. Title.
QB44.2.C57   1987   520   86-19848

ISBN 0-517-56245-6

10 9 8 7 6 5 4 3 2 1

First Edition

To Suzanne

CONTENTS

PREFACE
The Labors of Hercules

One of the Herculean achievements of humankind has been the conquest of space. In the realm of astronomy, the new understanding of the cosmos made possible from space far exceeds any comparable step forward in knowledge since the advent of the telescope almost four centuries ago. The remarkable achievements of recent years are likely to pale into insignificance, however, against the omniscience expected from a new generation of telescopes to be launched into space before the century's end. We are about to enter the era of the Space Telescope and the Space Station. Science fiction is about to become science fact.

The Cosmos from Space traces the evolution of our understanding of the universe that has been made possible using scientific instruments launched above the atmosphere on rockets and satellites. For example, X rays from celestial objects reveal sites of violent upheaval and change, in dramatic contrast to the relatively sedate universe observed in visible light using ground-based telescopes; infrared radiation locates the birthplaces of stars and planetary systems; other radiations also reveal objects and phenomena unobservable from the earth's surface and unknown (or even anticipated) prior to the advent of astronomy from space. On the basis of our new awareness of the nature of the universe, scientists can predict what might be discovered by the major new space observatories. Past experience would suggest that the cosmos will have plenty of surprises in store.

In a single volume, it would be quite impossible to do justice to all aspects of astronomy from space. A definitive history (yet to be written) of the birth of X-ray astronomy alone would occupy several volumes, yet in this book it has been summarized in just a single chapter. Clearly I have had to be extremely selective. In choosing material for inclusion, I found it necessary to restrict the science to the most spectacular, the technology to the most innovative, and the space missions to the most successful. No doubt my lists of scientific highlights, innovative technology, and successful space missions would differ markedly from those of others who have worked in space research during its first quarter century. Others might also have selected different possibilities for discoveries anticipated from the future space observatories. Crystal-ball gazing is never easy in astronomy: few of the most spectacular discoveries of the past were predicted. Despite the need to be selective and predictive, I hope I have been able to project some of the excitement of astronomy from space. I hope the reader will be able to appreciate the quite remarkable contributions to our understanding of the cosmos that have been made possible in the few decades since we broke the gravitational chains that bound us to Earth's surface, and to enjoy the speculation about what new discoveries future decades might bring.

I wish to thank my agent, Felicia Eth of Writers House, and my editors, Lisa Healy and Jake Goldberg. Most of all, I thank my family for their encouragement, and especially my wife, Suzanne, for all her love and help.

PROLOGUE
The Legacy of Ares

In the final days of World War II, the United States Army, unbeknown to its allies, surreptitiously evacuated 300 freight-car loads of captured German rocket parts from an underground factory near Nordhaussen (now in East Germany), just days before the region was due to pass to Soviet control. These relics of the mighty German war machine were shipped to El Paso, Texas. At the nearby White Sands military test range, spanning the Texas–New Mexico border, the first atomic bomb, Trinity, had been exploded just a few weeks earlier. Along with the captured military technology came the human spoils of war. German scientists, led by Wernher Von Braun, were set to work on further rocket development to complement the nascent U.S. missile technology based on the prewar pioneering research of Robert H. Goddard.

The early rockets tested from the White Sands range in 1946 were refurbished V-2s, the second of the German "vengeance" weapons (*Vergeltungswaffen*); almost 4,000 of these horrific tools of mass destruction had showered onto liberated Europe and southern England during the final months of the war, but too late to affect its outcome. Now the "swords of war" were being beaten into the "plowshares of peace," as scientists were given the opportunity to fly scientific instruments high into the atmosphere. The military, eager to develop rocket technology, was nevertheless willing to have the unarmed test rockets used for scientific research. The vacant half-cubic-meter V-2 warhead compartments were quite adequate to house pioneering scientific instruments for direct measurements of the upper atmosphere and for observations of hitherto hidden astronomical phenomena.

Until 1946 almost all we knew about the universe had been gleaned from the optical light radiated by the stars and galaxies (giant conglomerates of stars) and visible to the human eye, albeit usually aided by a telescope. But other forms of "invisible" radiation exist—gamma and X rays, ultraviolet and infrared radiation, micro- and radio waves. All these different forms of radiation are emitted by various cosmic objects and phenomena, and technology has provided the means to extend the human senses to detect the invisible radiations. However, gamma and X rays and ultraviolet and infrared radiation cannot penetrate the earth's atmosphere to be observed by earth-bound telescopes. Only optical and radio astronomy (and some infrared astronomy) can be carried out from the ground. Thus, even if it had been expected (which it had not) that certain cosmic objects and phenomena could generate other forms of radiation, the means just did not exist prior to 1946 to get instruments high above the atmosphere to detect them. (Balloons had been used to carry instruments only to relatively low altitudes.) All this was to change as the first scientific instruments were launched to high altitudes on rockets. The new wartime technologies were to herald a major revolution in our understanding of the heavens. The legacy of Ares, god of conflict, was to be transformed into the vision of Athene, goddess of wisdom.

Although the spoils of real war had assisted the advent of space research, it received its greatest boost from the hysteria of the Cold War of the fifties and sixties. When the Soviet Union launched the first artificial earth satellite, *Sputnik 1*, on October 4, 1957, the impact on U.S. national pride and Western confidence was devastating, as anyone who lived through that epoch-making event will readily recall. In the West, *Sputnik* was seen as the Pearl Harbor of the technology war. The propaganda effect of the U.S.S.R. space spectaculars dealt a severe blow to U.S. prestige, and a crash program was undertaken to close the missile gap. Control of the Space program was passed from the U.S. military to a newly created civilian space agency, NASA (the National Aeronautics and Space Administration); the military remained extremely active in missile development, however, and supported certain space-science projects. Each new shiver in the Cold War, failure in foreign policy, or Soviet space achievement seemed to be matched by a renewed injection of funds as the United States strove to "regain the high ground." An eventful week was that starting on April 12, 1961, which saw both the flight of Yuri Gagarin (first man in space) and the Bay of Pigs debacle—two events that seriously jolted the pride and confidence of a nation and its president, John

F. Kennedy. In such a political climate of tarnished national dignity, the charismatic young leader was able to persuade Congress to back the challenge of placing a man on the moon and returning him safely to Earth before the end of the decade. It was the unique concatenation of political circumstances and emerging technical capability, rather than scientific need, that gave birth to the moon program. Federal support for space exploration soared to billions of dollars annually. The space race was envisaged as the catalyst that would reestablish the global preeminence of U.S. science and technology; and so it proved. Space research was not limited to the superpowers, however. The space club rapidly gained new members: Britain, France, Germany, Italy, the Netherlands, India, Japan, and China. The Europeans combined their science resources into the European Space Research Organization (ESRO) and their rocketry aspirations into the European Launcher Development Organization (ELDO), amalgamated in 1974 into the European Space Agency (ESA).

Space research embraces many facets—adventure, political posturing, science, engineering, communications, monitoring of the earth's resources and weather patterns, military surveillance, specialized manufacturing processes, medical research, etc. Clearly, astronomers stood to benefit from the enormous injection of funds into space in its various guises (particularly the moon program) during the early years, and satellites carrying gamma-ray, X-ray, and ultraviolet detectors were soon launched into orbit. The pioneers of space research were principally engineers, or researchers moving from other scientific disciplines. Before long, however, traditional astronomers, trained in ground-based techniques, were attracted to the spectacular and unexpected discoveries being made from space. Today, space astronomy is still in its infancy, and the great cosmic spectaculars involving massive observatories in space are just starting—yet the advances in our understanding of the universe in the time since the first tentative steps by astronomers into space have been unmatched by any other period of scientific endeavor.

The Renaissance left as part of its heritage great cathedrals and newly discovered continents; twentieth-century humankind will leave as part of its heritage giant space stations ("cathedrals in the sky") and newly discovered "cosmic continents." The "new universe" revealed since the advent of space astronomy is the subject of this book.

1
HIGHWAY TO ZEUS

Men AND WOMEN HAVE ALWAYS VIEWED THE HEAVENS WITH awe, sensing the vastness of space, the power of the creation, and perhaps even something of their own origins, as they looked out into the clear night sky and the distant stars. Until the past few decades, however, they could have had no real appreciation of the true enormity of the universe, the cataclysmic nature of its origin, or their own close relationship to the stars. Yet scientists now put forward theories describing the evolution of the universe from a time just a fraction of a second after the creation—the "Big Bang" in scientific parlance. They claim that all the material of common experience, including the constituents of the organic compounds of which life forms are made, was forged in the interiors of stars from the simple atomic components of the early universe.

The vision of modern scientists extends from Earth's nearest, and comparatively well understood, planetary and stellar neighbors to bizarre and enigmatic objects at the very limits of the observable universe, accessible only with the most powerful instruments technology has been able to devise to extend the limited scope of the human senses. It extends from the origin of the universe, beyond its present turbulent state, to predictions about its ultimate fate. The scientist and layperson alike look out into the night sky, marvel at the wonders of the heavens, and ask themselves, What is our place in the universe? Where did we come from? How did it all begin, and how will it end?

Astronomy is one of the most ancient of sciences. Primitive peoples worshiped the celestial bodies and assigned them mystical powers, this worship eventually evolving into rational and systematic investigation. No changes in the positions of the stars with respect to each other were discernible to the unaided eye; the patterns formed by the brightest stars were identified as constellations, around which various fables and mythologies evolved. A false impression given by the remoteness of the stars is that they all lie at the same distance from Earth. Human eyes, separated by just a few centimeters, can perceive depth of field within distances of only a few hundred meters; they can't appreciate the vast range of distances to the stars. Only within the past century have accurate measurement techniques revealed the enormous distances to even the nearest stars, and only within the past few decades has science established the incredible size of the cosmos.

To set the scene for describing the contributions of space astronomy to our present understanding of the nature of the universe, we will undertake an imaginary tour of the heavens. To complete this guided tour, we will pretend that we have booked a journey on a spaceship of IGS (Intragalactic Spaceways). This spaceship is able to cruise at a speed of 3,000 kilometers per second—that is, at about 2,000 times the speed of a bullet, and quite beyond the capabilities of present or forseeable technology. (That is not to imply that one day, a century or more hence, the technology to achieve these, or even very much greater speeds, may not be achieved. In the early days of powered flight, an "ultimate" flying speed of 200 kilometers per hour was pronounced by certain "experts.") Let us not be deterred by reality, but instead pretend that such a futuristic spaceship exists. It could fly from London to New York in a mere two seconds or circumnavigate the globe in just twelve seconds. Yet even traveling at such incredible speeds (about 1 percent of the speed of light), we would have to be blessed with a remarkably long life to complete more than just the early stages of our imaginary celestial tour.

As we blast off from Earth, accelerating rapidly to our cruising speed, our first glimpse is of the moon, passed after just a few minutes, before the flight attendants have even had a chance to serve drinks and longevity tablets. We are heading away from the sun, out of the solar system. After seven hours we catch a brief glimpse of Mars; then three days later, after a breathtaking transit of the asteroid belt, we sight the largest of the planets of the solar system, Jupiter, with its orbiting moons—a solar system in miniature. By now we are starting to get used to the time scales involved between the major tourist sights; fortunately we have come well prepared with plenty of reading material. After three weeks of flying we pass beyond the orbit of the minuscule planet Pluto; we have left the solar system, and we set our course for the nearest star, Proxima Centauri, in the constellation commemorating the mythical man-horse. Our pilot announces an ETA some 430 years hence! Such is the great distance to even the *nearest* star, which if we were to measure its distance in units familiar on the terrestrial scale, would be at about 40 trillion kilometers. On the celestial scale, because of the vast distances involved, astronomers find it more convenient to introduce a unit of distance called the light-year. The light-year is the distance traveled by a pulse of light in one year (the speed of light is about 300,000 kilometers per second) and is equivalent to almost 10 trillion kilometers. Thus Proxima Centauri's distance, measured in this way, is 4.3 light-years. (A common mistake, made all too often by science-fiction authors and television scriptwriters, is to refer to the light-year as if it were a span of time rather than of distance.)

Stars are not uniformly scattered throughout space but accumulate in giant conglomerates called galaxies, each containing billions of stars. The most casual glance at the night sky reveals the concentration of stars along the thin band encircling the heavens known as the Milky Way. The Milky Way is our galaxy, the galaxy within which our solar system lies. Along the Milky Way the concentration of stars is so great that their light appears to merge into a nebulous band, pictured in mythology as the pathway to the home of the supreme god, Zeus. The sun and Proxima Centauri are among an estimated 100 billion stars making up the Milky Way. The Milky Way is discus-shaped, 100,000 light-years in diameter, with our solar system lying about midway between its center and periphery; it is one of the outer "suburbs" of our galaxy, far from its heart. Our sun turns out to be rather an insignificant star, in an unnoteworthy corner of a rather ordinary galaxy—hardly the preeminent position at the center of the universe as claimed by pre-Renaissance scholars!

Our spaceship's automatic navigation system is programmed to take us along "Zeus's highway" toward the center of the Milky Way, some 30,000 light-years away. Our pilot radios details of the course change to Earth Base; he must wait 10 years for a reply. Closing *The Complete Works of William Shakespeare* after a 300th reading, we settle back to watch our 100,000th in-flight movie. We have an exciting trip ahead, since the Milky Way isn't populated merely with sunlike stars and planetary systems. Surprises in store will include stars many times more massive than our sun, belching

The Milky Way

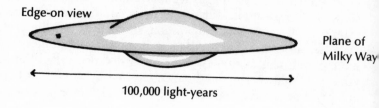

Edge-on view

Plane of
Milky Way

100,000 light-years

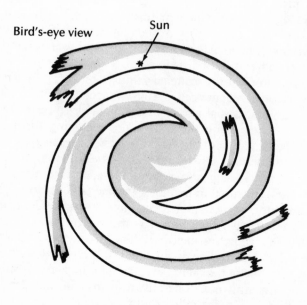

Bird's-eye view

Sun

their outer layers into space; minute, superdense stars (just a few kilometers across) rotating tens or even hundreds of times each second; star systems ejecting matter through finely collimated jets like giant garden sprinklers; stars at birth and stars in their death throes; stars orbiting each other and exchanging matter via a swirling disc; stars in isolation and stars in massive swarms; dense clouds of dust and gas and spectacular nebulosities. The heavens will display themselves in an almost infinite variety of exciting objects and phenomena. The glossy pictures in the IGS tour brochure had not been able to do justice to such a wonderland.

Stars come in a variety of forms, but those rather like our own sun might be described as typical; at least they are the variety encountered most frequently. A star is a fiery sphere of gas, some millions of kilometers in diameter. The visible surface of a star, referred to as its "photosphere," is at a temperature of several thousand degrees, and its internal temperatures are at millions of degrees! Within the Milky Way the majority of stars are not too different from the sun in the way they are formed and the way they evolve—although more exotic species certainly exist.

Some stars appear to be much brighter than others. In part, this is due merely to a difference in distance, the more distant stars appearing fainter; but it also reflects a wide range in the intrinsic brightness of stars. The system used to measure the brightness of stars is the so-called magnitude scale, adapted from a system originally introduced in 130 B.C. by the Greek astronomer Hipparchus. Hipparchus compiled the first catalog of stars, in which he listed their brightness on a scale of 1 to 6 (1 designating the brightest stars). This system was eventually quantified as follows: Negative numbers indicate a greater brightness than positive numbers, and each magnitude is 2.5 times brighter than the next one. Thus a fifth-magnitude star is 2.5 times brighter than a sixth-magnitude star, and so on. The observed magnitude of a star from Earth is called its apparent magnitude. For example, zero apparent magnitude is the brightness of the star Vega, and -4 apparent magnitude is the maximum brightness of the planet Venus. Actually, to make a meaningful comparison between stars, we need to know what their magnitudes would be if they were all placed at a standard distance. The distance chosen, for reasons which need not concern us here, is 32.6 light-years. The magnitude of a star calculated as if it were at such a distance is termed its absolute magnitude. If the sun were at a distance of 32.6 light-years, it would appear as a fifth-magnitude star; that is, its absolute magnitude is $+5$. Because of its proximity to Earth, it has an extreme apparent magnitude of -26.

When viewed from Earth, stars "twinkle"; that is, the stellar images appear to dance about and vary in brightness. This is an effect due to turbulence in the earth's atmosphere and certainly not due to the twinkling of the stars themselves. Here on our IGS tour, out in the clarity of interstellar space, twinkling is no longer a problem; the distant stars appear as fine points of light, and the nearby stars we pass appear as brilliantly glowing spheres. Occasionally, material is seen to be belched from their surface—a case of stellar hiccups (stellar flares). The nearby stars are so bright that we need protective spectacles to view them.

The void between the stars is not a perfect vacuum but is permeated by tenuous gas and dust called the interstellar medium. This is the material from which future generations of stars, planetary systems, and life forms will be fused. The gas tends to be concentrated into clouds tens of light-years across and glowing in brilliant colors. These are the nebulae (from the Latin word for cloud). Our tour guide describes the origin of different types of nebulae as we pass them. They all have one thing in common— their sheer beauty. It is as if Zeus, armed with a palette of vivid pigments, had swept the heavens with strokes of a giant paintbrush.

One type of nebula, of more modest size than most, always has a bright central star, with the nebula surrounding it like a giant smoke ring. These are the so-called planetary·nebulae, which result from certain stars expanding dramatically at an advanced stage of their evolution and ejecting some of their outer layers. Our own sun is presently enjoying a state of stable middle age but will eventually, some 5 billion years hence, undergo such a fate. Its present diameter is about 100 times that of Earth, but it will eventually expand dramatically to swallow up the inner planets, Mercury, Venus, Earth, and Mars. It will become what is known as a red giant—a highly evolved star that has become unstable and bloated. A planetary nebula will be ejected; matter will be belched into space as the sun undergoes its death throes before collapsing back to a size no greater than that of Earth. This shriveled remnant of a once-glorious star is called a white dwarf. Since it is believed that 999 out of every 1,000 stars end their lives so ingloriously, it is hardly surprising that red giants and white dwarfs prove relatively common sights as we journey onward in the direction of the center of the Milky Way.

The most common form of nebulae are clouds of dust and gas (mainly hydrogen) illuminated by bright young stars lying within the clouds. Often within these hydrogen nebulae dark regions abound. These are dense cloudlets of dust that obscure the light of any background stars. It is within such dense cloudlets that new stars are most likely to be born; a hydrogen cloud is a colorfully decorated cosmic nursery!

The third type of nebulae have their origin in spectacular stellar explosions called supernovae. A star more massive than about 10 times our sun eventually evolves to a bloated super giant before

undergoing a dramatic act of stellar suicide at the end of its evolution, with the release of vast amounts of energy. All but the central
core of the star is blasted out into space at high speed, like shrapnel
from a bomb. But what a bomb! The energy released in a supernova has been estimated to be equivalent to that from the simultaneous explosion of some 10 octillion 10-megaton hydrogen
bombs; it is quite beyond human comprehension. The central core
of the dying star collapses to a state of extreme density, spinning
rapidly. It may emit pulses of radio waves many times per second
—hence its name, *pulsar*. A pulsar is a mere few kilometers across;
you could place several on Manhattan Island, if it could take the
weight: A small pebble of pulsar material would weigh a quadril-
lion tons!

One of the promised highlights of our tour is an excursion
through the expanding debris from an ancient stellar explosion—a
so-called supernova remnant. Some of the most spectacular nebulosities in the heavens are the remnants of supernovae; perhaps the
best known is the famous Crab Nebula. Supernovae themselves are
one of the hazards of interstellar travel, and the automatic horizon
scanner is programmed to keep a careful watch for any outburst.
Supernovae occur within the Milky Way about once every 20 years
on average—the likelihood of our encountering one nearby during
our travels is remote. However, supernova remnants are long-lived
(for hundreds of thousands of years), and it is our intention to fly
through one. It is day 100 million of our tour. (Thank goodness the
spaceship is well stocked with superlongevity tablets!) Just ahead of
us lies the remnant of a brilliant supernova viewed on Earth back
in the year A.D. 2006—the most brilliant stellar event ever witnessed by humankind, we are told. We are rapidly approaching the
entangled web of expanding debris at the periphery of the remnant,
a changing kaleidoscope of brilliant color. What a magnificent
sight—but we've been warned it is going to be a rough trip, so we
must marvel at this celestial wonder while we can.

Our first indication of rapid approach to the supernova remnant
is a dramatic increase in the number of cosmic-ray particles picked
up by the spaceship's radiation detectors. Cosmic rays are energetic
particles that permeate the whole of space—indeed, they are con-
tinuously bombarding the earth's atmosphere; the more energetic
are detected at ground level, and others by instruments on spacecraft. At least some cosmic rays have their origins in supernovae,
and so it is hardly surprising that an increased level is recorded as

we approach the remnant. Our flight doctor assures us there is nothing to worry about—our spaceship is well shielded, and the increased radiation levels should not cause alarm.

When a supernova explodes, a shock wave expands rapidly outward into interstellar space. A common example of a shock wave is the one that precedes an aircraft traveling supersonically, producing a "sonic boom." The shock wave from a supernova sweeps up the tenuous interstellar gas, like a snowplow sweeping up snow. The glowing swept-up gas and ejecta are seen as the beautiful nebula marveled at from afar. But now we are blasting our way through the nebula and, not surprisingly, experiencing a bumpy ride. The fiery spectacle outside our windows quite takes our minds off any physical discomfort. Now we are through the nebula, to the calm interior of the remnant, and there at its center is the rapidly spinning neutron star, a pulsar whose beam of radio emission sweeps rapidly around the sky like a lighthouse beacon. The spaceship's radio monitors are tuned to receive its subsecond pulses, causing both amusement and fascination as we sweep past this still-beating "heart" of a dead star.

During our cosmic tour, we are not limited to studying just those objects that we pass nearby. The spaceship's observation deck is well stocked with telescopes, available at a modest fee. Perhaps the most glorious sights through the telescopes are star systems lying far beyond the Milky Way—independent galaxies which, like our own, contain billions of stars, gas, dust, and nebulae. Galaxies come in various shapes and forms. Some are of a complex spiral form, looking like gigantic pinwheels rotating sedately in space. Others are egg-shaped, the so-called elliptical galaxies. Finally there are the irregular galaxies, which seem to have no preferred form. Our Milky Way is a spiral galaxy. Galaxies tend to congregate in clusters containing from tens to thousands of galaxies. Clustering seems to occur around mammoth voids in the cosmos that are empty of any galaxies.

Many galaxies are seen to be sites of violent upheaval and change, particularly near their centers. These are the so-called active galaxies. The energy being generated in such active galaxies almost defies comprehension. Galaxies are often seen to be interacting—"cannibal galaxies" consuming unsuspecting "missionary galaxies." One of the more bizarre types of active galaxy is the so-called quasar. Quasars are objects at vast distance but of staggering intrinsic brightness, so that they can be detected even at the

Telescopes

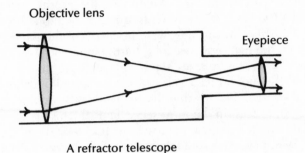

A refractor telescope

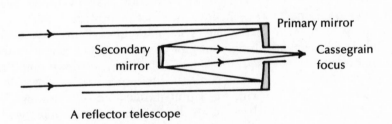

A reflector telescope

extremities of the observable universe. While the true nature of quasars is still poorly understood, they may be galaxies at an early stage of evolution, with a central "powerhouse" releasing energy at a prodigious rate.

Telescopes can use either lenses (refractor telescopes) or mirrors (reflector telescopes) to focus light. The ability of a telescope to distinguish objects close together is called its resolution. From the earth's surface, the resolution of a telescope is limited by the perturbing effects of the atmosphere, which smudges out images (an effect called astronomical seeing). Once in space, however, visibility is perfect, and the resolution of a telescope (its ability to pick out fine detail) is limited only by its size (the bigger the telescope the better its resolution) and the quality of its optics.

It is important to stress that in looking out into the cosmos through a telescope, one is looking not only deep into space but also back in time. Thus, because of the finite speed of light, the telescope acts as a "time machine," observing the nearby stars as they were just a few years or tens of years ago, and the more distant stars within the Milky Way as they were hundreds of thousands of years ago, when the light now reaching Earth commenced its cosmic journey. The nearby galaxies appear as they were millions of years ago, and the more distant galaxies as they were hundreds of millions of years ago. Few of the objects would still exist at the instant observed, at least in the form seen. Thus the history of the universe is laid out before us. Of course, our IGS tour is confined to the Milky Way; nevertheless, a telescope on the observation deck represents a magic carpet from which we can explore distant galaxies. The universe reveals itself as an unfolding drama.

It is intriguing that few stars occur in isolation (it has even been suggested that our own sun has a still-to-be-detected companion). Often stars exist in clusters of thousands, like swarming bees around a honey pot. Sometimes they occur in pairs, two stars orbiting each other in a binary system. Binary systems have been observed frequently during our tour. A common spectacle is material from the larger star in a binary system swirling down onto the surface of its smaller companion—like water flowing down the drain of a bathtub with the tap at the far end left running. In binary star systems where the smaller companion is a white dwarf, violent eruptions on the surface of the white dwarf may occur as more and more material from the larger star flows onto it. Such eruptions are called novae. Novae occur much more frequently than supernova explosions but are much less energetic.

Occasionally in binary systems the companion star is invisible, the material from the larger star swirling down an unobservable drain. Our flight attendant informs us at our first sighting of this bizarre phenomenon that the invisible star is a black hole.

The idea of a black hole can be explained in part by a simple thought experiment. When a ball is thrown into the air, it falls back to earth under the action of the earth's gravitational field. In the weaker gravitational field of the moon, there would be no difficulty in throwing the ball very much higher. If the ball could be thrown fast enough, it might escape the moon's gravitational field completely and fly off into space. The minimum velocity needed to escape an astronomical body's gravitational field is known as its

A close binary system

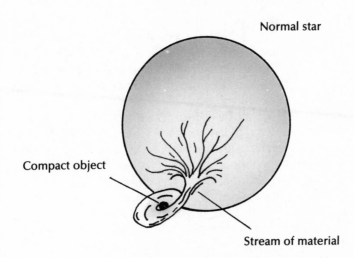

Normal star

Compact object

Stream of material

escape velocity. The escape velocity for the earth's surface is about 40,000 kilometers per hour. The more intense the gravitational field of an astronomical body, the greater its escape velocity. A white dwarf would have an escape velocity of several million kilometers per hour. If the escape velocity of a body exceeded the velocity of light (300,000 kilometers per second), then even light itself could not emerge from the body. Such is the nature of a black hole, an object invisible since its intense gravitational field does not allow even light to escape. *Nothing* escapes from a black hole —a black hole only consumes matter and never regurgitates it.

Where do black holes come from? It is likely that at least some come from very massive stars, many tens of times larger than our sun. Such a large, bloated star is extremely unstable, puffing off matter into space during its short, precarious existence, and its burned-out core eventually collapses to become a black hole.

Black holes, pulsars, white dwarfs, red giants, cosmic rays, and nebulae—stars at their birth and stars in their death throes—single stars, binary stars, and star clusters: What a tour it has been! But this is just the IGS minitour, planned to last a mere million years.

So, less than a fifth of the distance to the center of the Milky Way, we turn for home, having sampled just a few of the jewels of the cosmos. The IGS grand tour, all the way to the temple of Zeus at the heart of the Milky Way, must await another day.

Our imaginary tour of the Milky Way has set the scene. Now we know a little of what is out there, some of the different types of stars and star systems, galaxies and galaxy systems. But *why?* Where did it all come from? How did the universe begin and what will be its fate? The study of the grand structure of the universe, its origin and evolution, is called cosmology.

The world's religions all have picturesque accounts of the creation and predictions for Judgment Day. Historically, science has had no shortage of picturesque accounts either; indeed, there were usually rather more theories than there were facts to base them on. But twentieth-century astronomy has produced a wealth of evidence on which to base a sound scientific theory of the creation. Cosmology now claims that the origin of our present universe was heralded by the Big Bang—the cataclysmic release of matter and energy from which the stars and galaxies were formed.

If one were asked to name the single major contribution to our current understanding of the origin of the universe, it would have to be the observations that led to the realization that the universe is expanding. The detective work that led to this conclusion divided the scientific world and precipitated one of the great debates of modern times. All the galaxies were found to be receding from the Milky Way at enormous speeds, and the more distant they were the greater the speed of recession. This did not suggest that the Milky Way was at the center of the expansion (and consequently at the center of the universe!), but rather that it was merely part of a general expansion, so that all other galaxies thus appeared to be in relative recession from it.

If the galaxies are all receding from each other, then it is obvious that there must have been a time when all the matter of the universe was closely packed. We can try to estimate when this was by pretending to run back the present expansion, as though we were running a movie backward. If the expansion has proceeded uniformly, then 10 to 20 billion years ago all the material of which the universe is now composed must have been closely compacted. Thus, 10 to 20 billion years ago, the Big Bang of creation blasted the compacted universe to smithereens.

It is wrong to visualize matter released in the Big Bang as being

All galaxies are receding from one another as the universe expands.

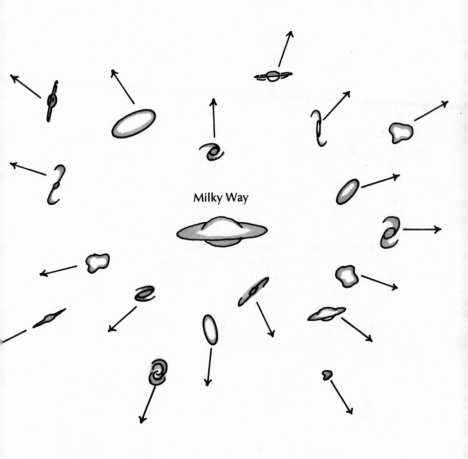

Milky Way

hurled out into a void—an empty-space universe that already existed. The expanding universe envisaged by modern cosmology is a true expansion of space itself, not just an expansion of the material substance of the universe. Thus the Big Bang initiated the universal expansion of *space*; the matter released in the Big Bang was forced to follow this expansion. In the process, matter was randomly accumulated under the action of gravity to form the galaxies of stars we now see receding from us. It is space itself that continues to expand, dragging the material universe with it. Today sensitive measuring instruments can still detect the weak remnant background radiation from the Big Bang—the faint echo of the creation.

What existed before the Big Bang? Perhaps the present universe was created from the burned-out cinders of some previous universe. Perhaps our own universe is but one of many miniuniverses within some grander but unobservable cosmos. We do not know. Another unanswered question is, what, or who, initiated the creation? Whose was the "hand" on the "plunger" of the Big Bang? But such questions are beyond the scope of science, which is concerned with making predictions based on patterns of behavior within the *observable* universe. The unobservable is not open to scientific interpretation and must therefore be ignored by science. Rather, such questions lie within the realm of the philosopher or the theologian—or the science-fiction writer! But science legitimately can, and does, speculate about the evolution of the universe and make predictions about its possible fate, based on current observations.

The expansion of the universe may be slowing down, very gradually, under the action of gravity. It is gravity, the universal attractive force between all matter, that holds the moon in orbit about the earth, the earth and other planets in orbit about the sun, and the sun and other stars in orbit about the center of the Milky Way. Although it is considered weak within the terrestrial domain, on the universal scale it is gravity that forms the stars, shapes the galaxies, and binds them in clusters.

Will the expansion of the universe continue forever, or will gravitational attraction between the clusters of galaxies eventually bring the expansion to a halt and indeed reverse it? The future behavior of the universe will depend on the density of the material within the universe, and this remains uncertain. Investigation of this problem is popularly known as the "missing-mass mystery." Only a small fraction of the material within the universe is trapped within the stars, the rest existing as tenuous gas and dust lying, often in clumpy clouds, between the stars (the interstellar medium), and between the galaxies (the so-called intergalactic medium). Much of this intergalactic and interstellar material is not visible to us, and it is the exact amount of this missing mass that will determine whether the expansion of the universe will eventually halt. If 99 percent of the mass of the universe is invisible, then eventually space will turn in on itself and the galaxies will be dragged toward each other in a universal contraction. Cosmologists speculate that such infall could eventually precipitate another Big Bang, as the galaxies are crushed together, giving birth to a new expanding universe out of the debris of the old. This is the basis of the "oscillating-universe" theory, in which a Big Bang and an expansion phase of the universe (lasting, it is conjectured, about 100 billion years) is followed by a contraction phase of equal duration, then the initiation of another Big Bang and the formation of a next-generation universe from the ashes of the old. This theory has the attraction of providing the universe with a permanency that requires no true beginning and no ultimate end but comprises merely a series of creative epochs punctuated by Big Bangs and interspersed with periods of expansion and contraction—a universe with an infinite future and an infinite past. One of the most pressing challenges to contemporary astronomy is to solve the missing-mass mystery—to decide whether the universe is "open," so that it will continue its presently observed expansion forever, or "closed" and possibly oscillating. Most bets are presently on an open universe, however philosophically difficult it might be to accept that we live in a universe that is gradually running down.

We must digress briefly to consider the structure of matter. The basic building blocks of all matter are atoms, the smallest recognizable components of the 92 known naturally occurring elements. Atoms themselves are composed of subatomic particles called protons and neutrons closely bound within a central nucleus, with minute electrons (a mere 2,000th of the mass of the protons or neutrons) orbiting the central nucleus. The electrons can move only in well-defined orbits of particular energy. To explore the realm of the atoms, let us pretend that we are able to take shrinking tablets that enable us to grow smaller. Each tablet shrinks our size to just a tenth of what it was before. Thus, after swallowing the first tablet we would be, say, just 18 centimeters tall, after the second tablet 18 millimeters, after the third just 1.8 millimeters, and so on. To shrink to the scale of an atom, we would need to consume 10 tablets, and to get down to explore the nucleus would require 15 tablets in all. If the diameter of a typical atom (defined by the size of its outer electron orbit) were scaled to the size of Chicago, its nucleus (containing the bulk of its mass) would be the size of a golf ball: Most of the volume of an atom is empty space!

It is the number of protons within the nucleus of an atom that identifies it as being that of a particular element. Thus, for example, the simplest elements are hydrogen and helium, with just one and two protons, respectively. Carbon atoms have 6 protons, oxygen 8, iron 26, copper 29, gold 73, lead 82, uranium 92, and so forth. In their so-called neutral state, atoms have the same number of orbiting electrons as they do protons within their central nuclei. The number of neutrons in an atom is usually about equal to or somewhat greater than the number of protons. Atoms of different elements can combine to form molecules. For example, a carbon-dioxide molecule is formed by the bonding of a carbon and two oxygen atoms.

In the seconds following the Big Bang, the universe must have been a dense soup of protons, neutrons, and electrons bathed in intense radiation—the original Dante's inferno. The temperature of billions of degrees was too extreme for the subatomic particles to combine to form atoms. Within a few minutes, however, the expanding celestial soup would have cooled to the point where protons and neutrons could combine singly to form deuterium nuclei (deuterium is a type of hydrogen; normal hydrogen has no neutron in its nucleus) and combine in pairs to form helium nuclei. Scientists conclude that within the first 15 minutes of its creation, 25 percent of the universe, by mass, must have been helium. It was to be at least a million years, however, before the universe had cooled to the point where electrons could combine with the hydrogen and helium nuclei to form true neutral atoms; this was the epoch of neutralization. The nascent universe was still almost entirely hydrogen and helium, with just a pinch of deuterium. The more familiar, heavier atoms still awaited their creation in the centers of the yet-to-be-formed stars.

Following the epoch of neutralization, galaxy formation commenced. Imagine a region of the evolving universe where the density of matter was slightly higher than elsewhere, so that it eventually underwent gravitational collapse as the universal expan-

Evolution of the universe

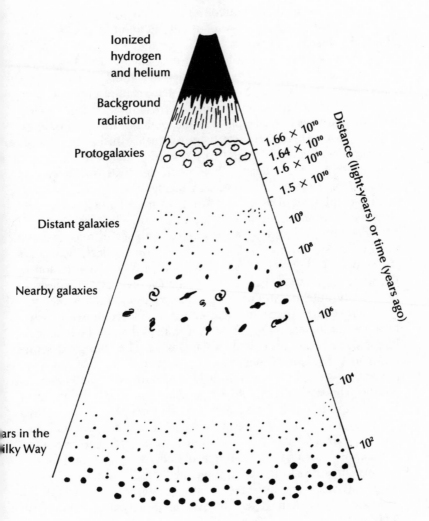

sion continued. As this so-called protogalaxy collapsed, it fragmented and the first generation of stars formed within the fragments. Gravity then organized the stars and remaining gas into the galactic forms we now observe, and organized the galaxies into clusters.

To follow the further evolution of the universe and the creation of the elements, we must now focus our attention on the evolution of individual stars.

As an isolated cloud of interstellar dust and gas (predominantly hydrogen and helium) collapses under the effect of gravity, the cloud heats up. Eventually it attains a temperature of tens of millions of degrees. At such extreme temperatures certain nuclear burning reactions can take place in the center of the collapsing gas cloud. These reactions are referred to as nuclear fusion. In a newly forming star, hydrogen nuclei in the core of the cloud are fused together to form the heavier helium nuclei, with the release of energy (referred to as thermonuclear energy).

The combined mass of the fusing hydrogen nuclei is *greater* than the mass of the resulting helium nucleus: The mass destroyed has been converted into energy. The equivalence of mass (m) and energy (E) is described by Einstein's equation $E = mc^2$, where c is the velocity of light. This is probably the best-known equation in the whole of science. Einstein's equation reveals that the destruction of a minute amount of mass creates a vast amount of energy.

The release of thermonuclear energy at the center of a newly forming star increases the internal pressure to the point where gravitational contraction is halted. A star is born! The young star settles down to the relatively stable state in which it spends most of its active life—fusing hydrogen to helium. During this long period of stability, the star's self-gravity acting inward is exactly balanced by the pressure pushing matter outward. This delicate stellar balancing act is maintained at the expense of the loss of nuclear fuel. In a star like our sun about 655 million tons of hydrogen are transformed into about 650 million tons of helium each second; the lost mass is converted to the energy eventually radiated from the star's surface. (Even using nuclear fuel at this rate, the mass of the sun will fall by less than 1 percent over its projected 10-billion-year lifetime.)

And so it is with all the stars. The loss of mass and the generation of thermonuclear energy provide the answer to the question that challenged human curiosity over the millennia, What makes

Evolution of a massive star

Star burns nuclear fuel
in its central core.

When all nuclear fuel is expended,
central core collapses.

An explosion is initiated—

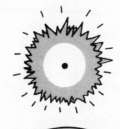

—observed as a supernova,
feeding enriched material
to the interstellar medium.

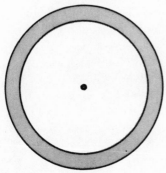

Thousands of years later,
expanding shell may be seen
as an extended supernova
remnant, and the collapsed
central core may be seen
as a pulsar.

the sun and stars shine? The energy source utilized with potentially catastrophic consequences in the building of thermonuclear (hydrogen) bombs is the very energy source successfully harnessed and controlled in the central furnaces of the stars.

Although the nuclear fuel reserves of a star are enormous, they are not unlimited. When the hydrogen in the central core of the star is expended, gravity again takes control. As the core starts to contract again it causes the internal temperature to increase to about the 20 million degrees needed to start the nuclear burning of the helium ash left over from the earlier hydrogen-burning phase. Helium nuclei fuse to form the heavier elements carbon and oxygen. When all the helium in the core is in its turn expended, later stages of nuclear burning may follow, involving the fusion of successively heavier elements all the way to iron, when no further reactions can extract energy.

Thus the long-sought-after goal of the medieval alchemist, to change the elements from one form to another, has indeed been achieved on the cosmic scale since the moment of creation. The heavier elements are then ejected into the interstellar medium when stars shed material during periods of instability in their evolution, and also of course in nova and supernova explosions. Indeed, in the extreme conditions of supernova explosions, certain heavy (rare) elements such as gold, silver, platinum, and uranium are formed. In fact, everything within our common experience had an ultimate cosmic origin, having been forged from primeval hydrogen and helium in the centers of the stars. Perhaps most sobering of all, the carbon, nitrogen, and oxygen of the organic compounds of which each of us is composed had its basic beginning in the stars eons ago. Ancient mythologies relating humankind to the stars thus contained a semblance of truth—we are indeed the "children of the stars," the "descendants of Zeus."

Interlude 1 • The Multicolored Cosmic Canvas

Radio waves, infrared radiation, visible light, ultraviolet radiation, X rays, and gamma rays are all forms of what are known as electromagnetic waves. These various types of radiation were discovered before the realization that they were all of a similar nature, traveling through open space with the same speed and differing only in their "color." As far as humans are concerned, the only thing special about visible light is that this is the most intense radiation from the sun that penetrates the earth's atmosphere, with evolution ensuring that it is the radiation to which the human eye is sensitive.

So, what is an electromagnetic wave? Let us start with familiar forms of waves. If one drops a pebble into a pond, one can see the ripples (or waves) propagating outward—it isn't the water spreading outward but merely the disturbance on the surface of the pond. The distance between the crests of the ripples is called the *wavelength*; the height of the ripples is called the *wave amplitude*; the speed with which the disturbance travels over the surface of the pond is the *wave speed*; and the number of ripples passing a fixed point each second is called the *frequency* of the wave. Another common example of a wave would be the disturbance in a stretched rope. If one end of the rope is fixed and the other end is flicked up and down, a wavelike disturbance will propagate along the rope, of certain wavelength, amplitude, speed, and frequency. Actually, the wavelength, speed, and frequency of a wave are related by a very simple formula: speed = wavelength × frequency.

That sorts out waves. But what does *electromagnetic* mean? A familiar example of an *electric* phenomenon is the childhood trick of rubbing a plastic comb and picking up small pieces of paper with it; an even more familiar example, of a *magnetic* phenomenon, is using a small magnet to pick up pins. Electric and magnetic phenomena can both be traced back to the subatomic particle, the electron, which has an inherent property known as electric charge. The charge of electrons is referred to as being negative; protons have positive electric charge. Materials that have an excess of electrons are said to be negatively charged, while those with a deficiency of electrons are positively charged. Bodies with the same type of electric charge repel each other, while oppositely charged bodies attract. Magnetic phenomena arise from electrons in motion.

The interaction between electrically charged bodies (such as the frictionally charged comb and pieces of paper) is ascribed to an electric field acting between them; similarly, the interaction between the magnet and pins is due to a magnetic field. In one of nature's more interesting (and important) symmetries, electric and magnetic fields are intimately linked. If an electric field is disturbed, it generates a magnetic field; if a magnetic field is disturbed, it generates an electric field.

So, back to dropping a pebble in a pond. The pebble disturbs the water, and this disturbance propagates outward as a water wave. Just as surely, if one disturbs an electric field the disturbance propagates outward as an electric wave; however, because of the close link between electric and magnetic fields, the electric disturbance is accompanied by a magnetic disturbance, constituting an electromagnetic wave.

It was a famous Scot, James Clerk Maxwell, who in 1865 developed the theory of electromagnetic waves. Maxwell's early theoretical considerations showed that if electromagnetic waves existed they would travel through free space with a speed of 300,000 kilometers per second, close to the best determined value for the speed of light available at the time. On the basis of this agreement, Maxwell suggested that light was a form of electromagnetic wave. As the other forms of radiation were discovered, they were in turn shown to be, like light, electromagnetic waves.

In fact, light is not emitted as a continuous wave but rather in small energy packets called photons. A stream of photons, however, can be modeled adequately as a continuous electromagnetic wave. If in an electromagnetic wave the electric component oscillates always in the same direction, the wave is said to be polarized; if

Schematic representation of an electromagnetic wave, made up of an electric wave (shaded) accompanied by a magnetic wave (unshaded) such that the electric and magnetic components are always at right angles.

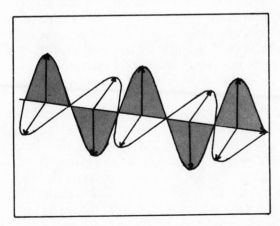

there is no preferred direction of oscillation the wave is said to be unpolarized.

It is the wavelength of an electromagnetic wave that determines its "color." The wavelength of red light is around 650 nanometers (a nanometer is a billionth of a meter). Green light has a wavelength of about 500 nanometers and violet light of about 400 nanometers. At wavelengths longer than red, we have infrared radiation (familiar to us as heat radiation). Beyond the infrared one enters the domain of radio waves; at short wavelengths (on the order of a millimeter) these are commonly referred to as microwaves. Radio waves extend to wavelengths of hundreds of meters, although they are most familiar (for the sending of radio and television signals) at wavelengths ranging from centimeters to a few meters.

At wavelengths shorter than visible light, one first passes through the ultraviolet region. At wavelengths shorter than 10 nanometers one is into the X-ray region, and then for extremely short wavelengths (less than a tenth of a nanometer) into the gamma-ray region.

One of the most familiar sources of electromagnetic radiation in the cosmos is, of course, the stars. A star emits electromagnetic radiation over a large range of wavelengths; the characteristic form

Energetic electron spiraling in a magnetic field produces
synchrotron radiation.

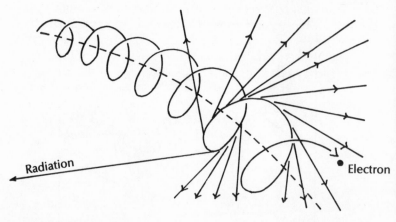

Radiation

Electron

Magnetic field

of this radiation depends very strongly on the surface temperature
of the star. And so it is with many other types of astronomical
objects. Cool bodies, such as dust clouds, planets, etc. (with
temperatures measured in hundreds of degrees), radiate principally
at infrared wavelengths. Stars have surface temperatures up to tens
of thousands of degrees; cooler stars are red and hotter stars are
blue, while hot stellar atmospheres (tens to hundreds of thousands
of degrees) radiate at ultraviolet to X-ray wavelengths. Thus, in
many astronomical situations, one can associate infrared and red
radiation with comparatively cool objects, and ultraviolet and X
radiation with hot, energetic phenomena.

One particularly important way whereby electromagnetic waves
are generated is called the synchrotron mechanism. A synchrotron
is a device for accelerating charged particles to high energies in
experiments in fundamental nuclear physics. When, in a
synchrotron, electrons are accelerated to very high speeds in a
magnetic field, they radiate electromagnetic energy at a variety of
wavelengths. This process also occurs in violent astronomical
phenomena where magnetic fields and particle acceleration exist,
such as active galaxies, stellar flares, and supernova remnants.
High-energy electrons spiraling along a magnetic field radiate X

rays and light, while those of low energy radiate at radio wavelengths.

The earth's atmosphere is opaque to most types of electromagnetic radiation. Only visible light and radio waves from the cosmos can be detected at sea level. Even for mountaintops, one gains access to only some infrared and microwave radiation. For most of the infrared and for the ultraviolet, X rays, and gamma rays, one needs to get instruments right above the atmosphere. The problem arises principally from absorption by the various gases that make up the atmosphere, including the minor constituents such as carbon dioxide, ozone, and water vapor. The atmosphere presents several other problems also. Perhaps the most obvious is cloud cover, which can be avoided in part by choosing a mountaintop observatory site in a temperate climate zone. Also, the atmosphere has a "brightness" all its own, due in part to the scattering of electromagnetic radiation from various sources (such as city lights, moonlight, auroral-type phenomena, lightning, etc.).

The transparency of the earth's atmosphere to electromagnetic radiation from space. (The light-shaded area depicts the opacity of the atmosphere as a function of wavelength.)

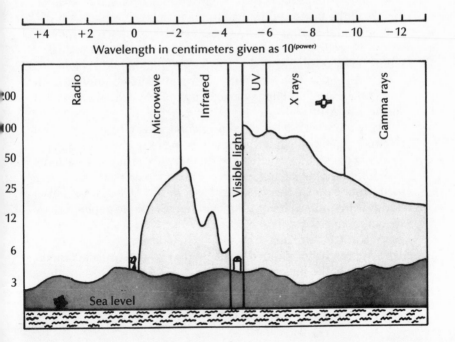

The atmosphere itself radiates at particular wavelengths (especially in the infrared). The detection of faint cosmic objects against this atmospheric background obviously presents a problem. It is clearly important to put a ground-based optical observatory as far as possible from sources of spurious light (such as a remote mountaintop, where altitude also provides a clearer atmosphere), but one cannot escape these sources entirely on the earth's surface. Radio observatories also need to avoid spurious emissions (interference from TV and radio stations, radar installations, car ignitions, etc.).

The atmosphere degrades the image of any celestial object. This arises from turbulence in the night air, causing the image of a star to twinkle. For an extended object (such as a galaxy or nebula) the sharpness of the image is lost. At high altitudes, and with an exceptionally stable atmosphere, visibility can be very good, but to avoid atmospheric distortion entirely one needs to get *above* the atmosphere into space.

From the ground, the celestial panorama available to an astronomer could be likened to the terrestrial panorama viewed with one eye closed, wearing tinted glasses, through thick fog. An artist would necessarily be limited if he were forced to use only black and white paint; nor can an astronomer produce an accurate picture of the heavens if limited to the radio and visible "paints" available on the ground. Astronomers *must* get telescopes into space, where there is a perfect "climate" (no clouds!), perpetual night, perfect visibility, and where background light can be limited to the feeble glow from the Milky Way and scattered sunlight from dust particles in the ecliptic plane of the solar system (the so-called zodiacal light).

There are several types of information that can be extracted from electromagnetic radiation that reveal something about its source. First, of course, there are images; these indicate the location and spatial form of the radiating object. Photographic plates have been used, until comparatively recently, as a means of acquiring and storing astronomical images; for certain uses, photographic plates are being superseded by sophisticated electronic detectors (particularly for working from space when data from electronic detectors can be transmitted to the ground for subsequent computer processing of the images). The second type of information is the total amount of light received from an object; this type of measurement is called photometry. A star's light may vary, and photometric observations will produce what is called a light curve —a plot of varying brightness with time. One can also study the polarization of electromagnetic waves from a cosmic object; not surprisingly, this is called polarimetry. Finally, there is spectroscopy.

It is well known that if a beam of white light passes through a slit and a prism, it is split into a rainbow of colors. The prism bends the different components of white light (red being bent least, violet most) into a merging row of colors called a spectrum. A practical spectrometer (a device used to produce a spectrum) normally uses a grating rather than a prism to disperse the light. Since white light produces a continuous range of colors, it is said to have a continuous spectrum. By contrast, the spectrum of some particular light source may show just selected features of different colors against a dark background. Such a spectrum is called an emission-line spectrum, each spectral line being an image of the slit-shaped instrument aperture in a single color. An emission-line spectrum is a unique characteristic of the radiating material, a fingerprint or signature that allows its unambiguous identification. If a beam of white light displaying a continuous spectrum shines on a low-density gas that does not itself radiate, certain colors of the incident light are absorbed so that the emergent light shows dark lines in its spectrum against a continuous background. Such a spectrum is referred to as an absorption-line spectrum. The colors of light absorbed are the same as those that would be emitted by the gas if it were made to radiate, so that an absorption-line spectrum of gas reveals the same information as would its emission-line spectrum. Since the spectrum of a particular light source provides important information on the composition, density, and temperature of the light source, spectroscopy, the study of spectra of different sources of electromagnetic radiation, has proved to be an extremely powerful technique in astronomical observations from space.

Spectroscopy is also important in determining the velocity of a light source, through a phenomenon known as the Doppler effect. The most familiar manifestation of this phenomenon is the change of pitch noticed by a stationary observer when a source of sound approaches and passes. Thus, for example, when a police car approaches with its siren on, the sound waves are "bunched up" ahead of it (in the sense that the distance between adjacent sound-wave crests is shortened, that is, the wavelength is decreased and the sound is of higher pitch than when the siren is stationary).

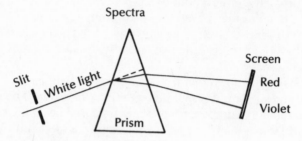

Continuous spectrum

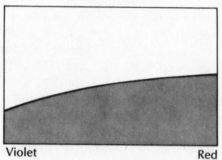

Emission-line spectrum

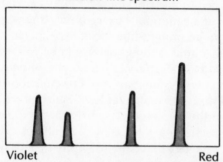

Absorption-line spectrum

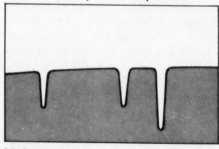

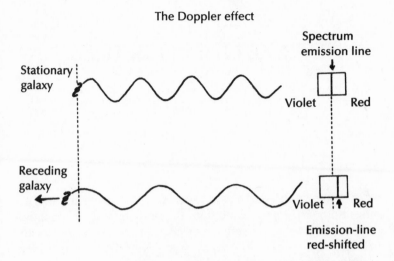

The Doppler effect

Stationary galaxy

Spectrum emission line

Violet   Red

Receiving galaxy
Receding galaxy

Violet   Red

Emission-line red-shifted

When the source of sound is receding, the waves are "stretched out" (in the sense that the distance between adjacent wave crests is lengthened), thereby increasing the wavelength and making the pitch lower. As it is with sound waves, so it is with light waves. If a source of light (for example, a star or a galaxy) is approaching an observer, the wavelength (defining the "color") of any characteristic emission is decreased; the light is said to be blue-shifted (emission features shift toward the blue end of the spectrum). When the source is receding, the light is red-shifted. The greater the speed of approach or recession, the greater the degree of blue shift or red shift. Thus the measurement of wavelength shift (compared with a laboratory source) provides the velocity of the source along the line of sight.

The story of our present cosmic quest involves the most sophisticated instruments technology has been able to devise to extend the limited scope of the human senses. Futuristic spacecraft now probe the depths of space for radiations that could never be observed from the earth's surface, complementing observations from the ground in producing a "multicolored" panorama of the universe. The cosmic canvas may never be completed, however, since the true complexity of the universe may be beyond the ultimate capability of human understanding. Nevertheless, our attempts to understand the nature of the universe must surely represent one of the great human challenges.

——— 2 ———
THE PRIZE OF PROMETHEUS

ARGUABLY THE MOST SPECTACULAR AND UNEXPECTED DIS-coveries from space have come from the study of X rays emanating from a wide variety of celestial objects. It is surprising to recall, therefore, that until 1962 X-ray astronomy had been widely thought to hold little promise. There had been various ideas put forward for possible sources of celestial X rays, such as supernova remnants and active galaxies, but these ideas had seemed to some scientists to be rather speculative. X rays, perhaps best known to the layperson for their use in medical diagnosis, are a highly energetic and penetrating form of radiation; if X rays were generated in the cosmos, it was argued, they must come from sites of great energy and objects at extreme temperatures. Prometheus, son of the Titan Iapetus, stole the "fires of heaven" for humankind—would celestial X rays reveal the prize of Prometheus? X rays had been detected from the sun by early rocket payloads. Calculations showed, however, that if all stars radiated X rays with about the same intensity as the sun, the level of X rays reaching the earth from even the very nearest stars would be too weak to be detected with existing instruments. Detectors with a billionfold increase in sensitivity would be required.

In June 1958, in the aftermath of the first *Sputnik* launch, the United States National Academy of Sciences formed the Space Sciences Board to advise both it and the newly formed NASA. The board had 15 members, under the chairmanship of Lloyd V. Berkner; its task was to formulate a future space-science policy and to solicit proposals for space missions. The Astronomy Committee of the Space Sciences Board took account of the speculative suggestions of possible sources of celestial X rays and recommended that an all-sky X-ray survey be undertaken. The program was, however, given low priority by NASA, which was after spectacular discoveries and missions with a high public visibility. (Little did they realize then that some of the most spectacular space discoveries would come from this area they had initially placed at low priority; there is surely a lesson here for present and future generations of space planners. However, NASA was to have a change of heart in 1963.)

One of the popular myths of the recent history of science is that X-ray astronomy had its birth purely by accident. Stories abound of how a rocket payload prepared for a completely different purpose discovered, completely by chance, the first celestial source of X rays other than the sun. Like so much of "history," this story is based only very loosely on fact. Certainly, the first celestial X-ray source *was* detected by an experiment dedicated to a very different objective; however, the myth overlooks the extensive work done by small, dedicated groups of individuals who had argued the case for searching for various possible celestial sources of X rays and indeed had made detailed preparations for such searches.

To understand why there was uncertainty as to whether X-ray astronomy would prove fertile, one must disgress to look at the state of astronomy before the commencement of the space era. By the mid-1950s the evolution of ordinary stars was thought to be reasonably well understood. Fusion of hydrogen to helium was recognized to be the certain primary source of the enormous energy of the sun and other stars; Lord Rutherford had first transmuted atomic nuclei by bombardment at the Cavendish Laboratory in Cambridge, England, and his Cambridge colleague Sir Arthur Eddington had wryly observed, "What is possible in the Cavendish Laboratory may not be too difficult in the sun." The detailed nuclear processes by which stellar energy is generated by the fusion of hydrogen to helium were formulated in the late 1930s by Hans Bethe (later a leading theoretician in the Manhattan Project to develop the atomic bomb) and others. In the early 1950s, in one of the monumental contributions to stellar astrophysics, the theoretical basis of the more complex reactions leading to the production of heavier elements in stellar interiors was investigated by Fred Hoyle of Cambridge and William Fowler of the California Institute of Technology. (Fowler subsequently received the Nobel prize in part for his contribution to this work; strangely, Hoyle's contribution was not recognized.) While the evolution of normal stars was thought to follow reasonably well understood and comparatively stable paths, it was realized that the death throes of stars in supernova outbursts did produce vast outbursts of energy and conditions of extreme upheaval.

Much of what is known about the sun and other stars has been gleaned from spectroscopy. As already noted, a spectrum of any light source is a characteristic signature that uniquely identifies the elements emitting the light. Since antiquity it has been recognized that there is an extensive faint "halo" surrounding the sun, known as the corona; the solar corona is visible to the unaided eye only during the short period of a total solar eclipse. (Even at eclipse, of course, the sun should be viewed only through a suitable filter.) The spectrum of the solar corona defied an exact interpretation until 1942, when it was realized that it must originate in matter at millions of degrees (in stark contrast to the temperature of the visible surface of the sun which is on the order of 6,000 degrees). At such extreme temperatures, X rays should be produced; thus, the solar corona would be expected to emit X rays.

Another thread of the story comes from an unexpected source, the history of radio transmission. The first major demonstration of radio was, of course, made in 1901 by the Italian-born inventor Guglielmo Marconi, who transmitted messages over the 2,700 kilometers from Cornwall, England, to Newfoundland, Canada. But how was this possible, when the curvature of the earth should have prevented the radio waves from reaching their destination? An explanation was quickly proposed independently by the American Arthur Kennelly and the Englishman Oliver Heaviside. They suggested that the radio waves were being bounced off a reflecting layer in the upper atmosphere. The nature of this layer was that atoms in the atmosphere had somehow been stripped of their electrons, becoming ionized; one means by which atoms can be ionized is by energetic photons. Such an ionized layer in the upper atomsphere would reflect the radio waves incident on it, allowing them to be transmitted around the curvature of the earth. The reflecting layer was known initially as the Kennelly-Heaviside layer, not the easiest of names to get one's tongue around. In 1929 Robert Watson-Watt (later one of the inventors of radar) introduced the simpler term retained to this day, the *ionosphere*. Direct probing of the ionosphere was an early objective of rocket research.

If an ionosphere existed, then what was the source of the radiation that ionized the upper atmosphere? The most likely culprit, the sun, was quickly identified, and the diurnal and seasonal variations in the properties of the ionosphere confirmed the link. One of the research laboratories that pioneered ionospheric research was the Naval Research Laboratory (NRL), opened on the banks of the Potomac River in southwestern Washington, D.C., in 1923. Since the United States Navy needed to maintain long-distance radio communication with ships around the globe, their interest in the behavior of the ionosphere was hardly surprising; in fact, this interest would mean eventually their taking a leading role in the development of X-ray astronomy. An NRL ionosphere pioneer was Edward Hulburt, who was the first scientist to propose, in 1938, that X rays from the sun were responsible for producing the ionosphere.

If the origins of X-ray astronomy are appearing diffuse already, then additional patience is required as we digress further.

In the early part of this century, there was still some uncertainty as to whether the universe extended beyond the Milky Way. There was certainly no consensus about the true size of the Milky Way. This was all to change with the work of Harlow Shapley. Shapley was in many ways an unlikely candidate for someone who would revolutionize our understanding of the cosmos. He had started his working life as a crime reporter for a small-town newspaper in Kansas, where *crime* meant mainly the fights of drunken oilmen. Wishing to better himself, he entered the new University of Missouri to study journalism. Unfortunately, the journalism course was not available as promised, and essentially by accident Shapley ended up enrolling in astronomy. As he himself described it, "I opened the catalog of courses. . . . The very first course offered was a-r-c-h-a-e-o-l-o-g-y, and I couldn't even pronounce it. . . . I turned over the page and saw a-s-t-r-o-n-o-m-y, I *could* pronounce that— and here I am." (It is surprising to learn how many other greats of astronomy entered the discipline purely by chance.) Shapley's research on clusters of stars in the Milky Way, and in particular variable stars called RR Lyraes, which are found in clusters, showed that the star clusters were scattered throughout a flattened spherical volume with a diameter of about 100,000 light-years. No one had previously appreciated the true size of the Milky Way. Perhaps even more sobering, Shapley's work placed the solar system about 30,000 light-years from the center of the Milky Way. The rather insignificant setting of our sun could be appreciated for the first time.

Just before the turn of the century, the great telescope builder George Ellery Hale founded the Yerkes Observatory of the University of Chicago, with its majestic 40-inch refractor telescope. He then moved on to California, where he established the Mount Wilson Observatory (with its 60-inch and 100-inch reflector telescopes) and the Mount Palomar Observatory (with its mighty 200-inch reflector telescope). An amazing feature of the construction of these big telescopes, which were to lead to so many of the monumental advances in astronomy, was that they depended very largely on personal patronage. Hale had persuaded a Michigan trolley-car magnate, Charles T. Yerkes, to fund his Chicago telescope. His first Mount Wilson telescope was funded by John D. Hooker, a Los Angeles businessman. Later Hale attracted support from Andrew Carnegie. Rumor has it that multimillionaire industrialist and philanthropist J. D. Rockefeller read only the first few sentences of an article written by Hale in 1928 for *Harper's* entitled "The Possibilities of Large Telescopes" before telephoning Hale with an offer of $6 million through the Rockefeller Foundation. This inspired patronage resulted in the construction of the 200-inch telescope at Mount Palomar, still one of the world's great telescopes. Today the scale of most (but certainly not all) astronomical projects, particularly from space, is such that they are beyond even the most generous of benefactors and depend instead on the collective patronage of the taxpayers of the developed nations. Personal patronage remains, however, a welcome bonus for astronomy.

It was the big telescopes in California in particular that were to revolutionize our understanding of galaxies. Various types of nebulae, and especially those displaying a spiral structure, had been studied in some detail since the eighteenth century. Some scientists felt that these could be independent galaxies lying far beyond the Milky Way (the concept of a universe made up of many galaxies had been alluded to in the mid-eighteenth century by the English scientist Thomas Wright and the German philosopher Immanuel Kant, who termed the nebulae "island universes"); but others thought they might be star systems within the confines of the Milky Way. The work of Edwin P. Hubble, using the big California telescopes, put the question beyond possible doubt. One of the giants of twentieth-century science, Hubble, like Shapley, arrived at a career in astronomy by a roundabout route. After obtaining a degree in science, he was awarded a Rhodes scholarship to Oxford, where he studied law. On returning to the United States, under paternal pressure he spent a short time practicing law. But his first love was science, and he obtained a doctorate in astronomy in 1917. He then turned down the opportunity to go directly into an astronomy career choosing instead to serve his country in World War I. Fortunately he was able to take up an appointment at the Mount Wilson Observatory a little more than a year later. Using the new 100-inch telescope he set about studying the spiral nebulae in great detail. Hubble's research proved conclusively that they were indeed independent galaxies at vast distances of millions to hundreds of millions of light-years—quite mind-boggling distances that put a scale to the universe never before imagined. Hubble's research established the basis for the present classification scheme for the different types of galaxies (spiral, elliptical, and irregular). Most startlingly, from Doppler measurements Hubble showed that the galaxies were all flying apart from each other at enormous speed, laying the conceptual foundation for the Big Bang model of the evolution of the universe.

Not all galaxies were found to be peaceful and quiescent systems. In 1943 Carl Seyfert discovered several spiral galaxies with hot gas being ejected from their nuclei at speeds of up to 1,500 kilometers per second, and it is now known that about 1 percent of spirals are Seyfert galaxies. The most convincing evidence for conditions of extreme violence in galaxies was to come, however, from the new science of radio astronomy.

Radio astronomy did arise by chance, in the experiments of Bell Telephone Laboratories radio engineer Karl Jansky, during 1931–32. Jansky was investigating the nature of radio noise, particularly that originating in thunderstorms, which interfered with communication by radio. In addition to noise of terrestrial origin, he recognized "a hiss in the phones that can hardly be distinguished from set noise." He was able to report that "radiations are received any time the antenna is directed toward some part of the Milky Way system, the greatest response being obtained when the antenna points toward the center of the system. This fact leads to the conclusion that the source of these radiations is located in the stars themselves or in the stellar matter distributed throughout the Milky Way."

Jansky's accidental discoveries passed unnoticed at the time by most of the astronomical fraternity, conditioned to believe that all the important secrets of the cosmos could be revealed in visible light. The postwar reemergence of radio astronomy was led by the new breed of wartime-trained radio engineers, skilled in the radio-direction-finding and radar techniques so easily adapted to radio astronomical investigation. The first discrete celestial radio-wave source was identified in 1946 in the constellation Cygnus and was designated Cygnus-A. By the late 1950s, extensive surveys of the radio sky had resulted in the publication of a series of catalogs of radio sources, and several associations of radio sources with optical objects had been proposed. Certain galaxies were found to be intense emitters of radio waves, the so-called radio galaxies. The nature of the radio emission suggested sources of extreme energy far beyond those indicated from optical observations. Within the Milky Way, the first source of radio emission identified was the remnant of a supernova (the Crab Nebula), again a phenomenon associated with violent upheaval. One of the most startling revelations of radio astronomy (with important assistance from optical astronomy) occurred in 1963, with the discovery of quasars (as already explained, these are believed to be the nascent galaxies at extreme distances, emitting energy at rates beyond anything previously thought possible in the cosmos). Radio astronomy was revealing a universe dramatically different from the vision of relative stability and tranquillity seen in optical light. On the scale of both stars and galaxies, high-energy processes were remolding the cosmos—just the conditions in which X rays might be expected to be produced. This evolving picture of a violent universe encouraged some scientists to argue that observations in X rays would become important as soon as the means became available to carry them out. There was consequently much speculation, theoretical investigation, and planning before the "accidental" birth of X-ray astronomy in 1962.

The first observations of celestial X rays occurred on August 5, 1948, when Robert Burnright of NRL inferred solar X rays from the darkening of a photographic emulsion carried aloft by a V-2 rocket. This first detection in fact merely confirmed the presence of X rays (presumably of solar origin) in the upper atmosphere. The definitive association with the sun was made by another NRL scientist, Herbert Friedman. Friedman was one of those directly responsible for the advent of X-ray astronomy, although his preeminent role has often been understated. Friedman, a quiet man, has never been one to stress the importance of his own pioneering role, in contrast to many others involved in X-ray astronomy during its early years. After gaining a doctorate from Johns

Geiger counter. A large voltage is placed across the electrodes. An X ray entering the tube via the mica window ionizes the gas in the tube (for example, argon). Electrons thus produced cascade toward the central electrode (ionizing other atoms as they go). A pulse of current is produced, which activates either a ratemeter or an amplifier and loudspeaker.

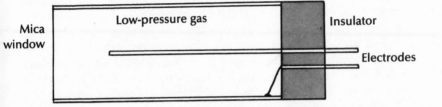

Hopkins, Friedman joined NRL in 1940. One of his early tasks was to develop compact X-ray counters for detecting the radiation emitted during atomic-bomb explosions. These were based on the venerable Geiger counter, a gas-filled tube with a thin window of suitable material that would block visible and ultraviolet radiation but would pass X rays. Working with Hulburt, Friedman decided to use his counters to search for solar X rays. Launched on a V-2 rocket on September 29, 1948, the counters detected intense X radiation when pointed toward the sun. The solar origin of the ionizing radiation was now indisputable; Hulburt's theory had been proved conclusively. By now Friedman realized that solar X-ray astronomy held enormous promise, and during the 1950s his NRL group maintained an undisputed lead in this field of research. Numerous rocket experiments, and later instruments flown on satellites, provided a detailed X-ray picture of the sun. As expected, the dominant X-ray feature was the corona, but solar flares (energetic outbursts from the solar surface) were also detected in intense X rays. Despite the high temperatures involved, however, these studies showed that the total X-ray intensity of the sun was extremely small. Only 1 millionth of the total energy emitted by the sun was in the form of X rays. There seemed little prospect of detecting coronal X-ray emission from even the nearest stars (assuming they had coronae like the sun) using X-ray detectors with the sensitivity then available or those under development. The NRL group did fly a number of rocket payloads in an attempt to detect extrasolar X rays, but without real success. Friedman was to reveal later that his group had obtained, as early as 1956, some puzzling results that might have been due to celestial X rays; unfortunately, they could not be absolutely certain since the detectors always also had the sun in their field of view. This all did not augur well for the future of X-ray astronomy. Nevertheless, the enthusiasts still felt motivated, by the radio evidence of extremely energetic celestial phenomena, to look for sources of X rays other than normal stars—for example, supernova remnants, certain types of peculiar stars, and active galaxies.

The importance of Friedman's early solar work must not be underestimated. It provided much of the innovative technology needed for the emergence of X-ray astronomy. Friedman would remain one of the principals of this major new field of research.

And so we come to the work of the man who would stand colossuslike astride the field of X-ray astronomy for two decades, Riccardo Giacconi. Giacconi is a person of enormous vitality and energy, which when coupled with self-confidence, technical competence, and leadership ability meant he was sure to succeed in any research field. Giacconi's mentor was Bruno Rossi, a professor at the Massachusetts Institute of Technology. Rossi was one of those who, despite the prospect of only feeble emanations from stellar coronae, was nevertheless advocating in the early 1950s that the exploration of the X-ray sky would prove a worthwhile endeavor. He had worked during the war on diagnostic techniques used in the development of atomic weapons and consequently had the technical skills to be attracted to the emerging postwar field of space research. An early interest was the study of the solar wind, the flux of energetic particles emitted from the sun and streaming through interplanetary space. But why the interest in X-ray astronomy? Well, why not? Experience had taught Rossi that probing previously unexplored fields inevitably produced entirely new and unexpected phenomena. Why should the X-ray universe be otherwise? How right he was!

Rossi had the opportunity to follow his instincts through American Science and Engineering (AS and E), a small company in Cambridge, Massachusetts, formed by two of Rossi's former MIT students, Martin Annis and George Clark. Rossi was made chairman of the AS and E board. Much of the company's early work arose from defense research contracts, but Rossi was a strong advocate for also pursuing innovative research in the technology required for X-ray astronomy. Riccardo Giacconi, a recent immigrant from Italy, was placed in charge of the AS and E X-ray astronomy program. It is unlikely that a more enthusiastic leader for the nascent research field could have been found; Giacconi happened to be the right person, with the right company, pursuing the right research program, at the right time. He was an example of a new breed of ambitious young professionals attracted to astronomy and space research in the late 1950s and the 1960s.

In 1959, Giacconi, Clark, and Rossi published an AS and E report entitled "A Brief Review of Experimental and Theoretical Progress in X-Ray Astronomy." This report looked at possible sources of celestial X-ray emissions—for example, very hot stars, stars displaying flaring phenomena, and supernova remnants. Particular reference was made to the last, and (in a remarkable piece of crystal-ball gazing) the Crab Nebula was identified as a source of special promise. Extrapolation of the weak emissions from the sun suggested to the AS and E team that dramatically improved detection methods were needed. Giacconi proposed a novel type of X-ray telescope to collect the maximum flux of X-ray photons and to focus them onto a conventional X-ray detector. Giacconi had read of the work in the late 1940s of German physicist Hans Wolter on the design of X-ray microscopes and speculated that Wolter's techniques could be employed in large X-ray telescopes. At X-ray wavelengths, a normal reflecting telescope configuration will not work: The X rays will pass through the mirror material without being reflected. However, X rays can be reflected at grazing incidence; that is, at very shallow angles of incidence. By using in conjunction parabolic and hyperbolic mirrors of extreme surface precision, X rays can be focused onto a suitable detector. Indeed, several mirrors can be nested concentrically to increase the total X-ray collecting power (this was Rossi's suggestion). Giacconi realized that such an X-ray telescope, feeding a Geiger-type counter of increased sensitivity, could detect the weak X-ray emission expected from cosmic objects. The AS and E report was submitted to various funding agencies, including NASA, in an attempt to promote support for exploratory work in X-ray astronomy. NASA did provide a contract, worth $216,000, to develop a prototype X-ray telescope, although it felt unable at that stage to fund a full X-ray astronomy mission.

The first conference on X-ray astronomy was a one-day event,

An X-ray telescope. X rays can be focused by causing them to reflect from specially shaped surfaces at grazing angles of incidence. In one type of X-ray telescope, the rays are reflected first from a paraboloid surface and then from a hyperboloid one.

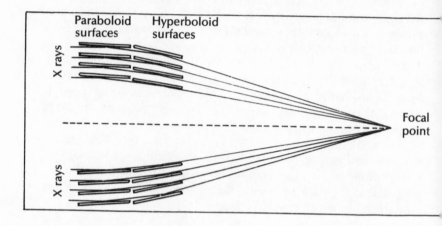

on May 20, 1960, at the Smithsonian Astrophysical Observatory in Cambridge, Massachusetts. The meeting attracted 24 scientists, all enthusiastic believers in the prospects for X-ray astronomy. Despite the likely weakness of stellar coronal emissions, it was hoped by those present that unanticipated sources might be very much brighter. Thus we can see that by 1960 the foundations for X-ray astronomy had been well and truly laid—its emergence was *no* accident. Despite the romantic notion that X-ray astronomy had an entirely serendipitous origin, an accurate history would reveal that its roots were deeper and wider than many other contemporary scientific research disciplines.

While pursuing the NASA X-ray telescope contract, the AS and E scientists considered a promising independent experiment that could use state-of-the-art instrumentation. They decided to look for X rays from the moon. It was believed that lunar X rays might be produced by two processes: First, solar X rays incident on the moon could cause X-ray fluorescence of the surface, and second, energetic electrons from the solar wind impinging on the lunar surface could produce X rays. The proposed experiment clearly reflected Rossi's interest in the solar wind and interplanetary phenomena.

Support for the lunar X-ray experiment was provided by the Air Force Cambridge Research Laboratories (AFCRL). Like the United States Navy, the United States Air Force supported various space activities; AFCRL had placed several research contracts with AS and E preceding their support for the lunar X-ray project. Funding was provided initially to fly a small AS and E X-ray-sensitive Geiger counter aboard an Air Force Nike-Arp rocket. The first attempt was a failure, because the rocket engine misfired. However, AFCRL's confidence in the AS and E group was demonstrated with a $120,000 contract for four flights on larger Aerobee rockets. Moreover, the enhanced contract made mention not only of the lunar experiment but also expanded the objectives to the detection of other sources of nonsolar X rays.

The availability of the larger Aerobee rocket meant that the AS and E scientists could be more ambitious with their instrumentation. Larger Geiger counters were developed, with sophisticated electronics that could discriminate the sought-after X rays from unwanted incident cosmic rays. The first launch of the new instrument was scheduled for October 24, 1961, from the White Sands test ranch. The launch was flawless. But to the dismay of Giacconi and his colleagues, the data telemetered to the ground failed to show any X rays. The reason was simple—the covers designed to protect their instrument through launch had failed to open! The scattered debris of what remained of the experiment was gathered from the desert. The rocket pioneers required a degree of patience and commitment demanded of few other scientists. Success had to wait for another day.

The second Aerobee launch was scheduled for the late evening of June 18, 1962. Again the launch was perfect. This time the protective covers did open successfully as the rocket blasted through an altitude of 200 kilometers. Although one of the three Geiger counters had failed on launch, the remaining two scanned the sky for a full six minutes before reentry. At last the experiment had operated successfully. An intense flux of nonsolar X rays had been detected. But was it the moon?

Detailed examination of the data showed that the strong detection was *not* from the moon but from a source toward the center of the Milky Way. Another, less intense source may also have been present, and a diffuse background radiation was detected throughout the flight. A thorough analysis failed to reveal even faint lunar fluorescent X rays, because of the confusing effects of the bright source and the background radiation. The experiment had thus failed in its primary objective but had succeeded beyond all expectations in detecting an intense celestial source of X rays. The faith of the dedicated few had been fully justified. The foresight of Rossi, the dedication of Friedman, the ambition of Giacconi—nature had rewarded them all. Here, indeed, was a new gift of the "fires of heaven" from Prometheus.

While the AS and E discovery was enormously exciting, its totally puzzling nature has to be emphasized. While the enthusiasts had proposed various possible sources of celestial X rays, nothing of the observed intensity had ever been suggested. If the detection was from a nearby star, for example, it would have to emit X rays at a prodigious rate some 10 billion times greater than the sun to explain the observed detection! Here, clearly, was a new and totally unexpected type of celestial object that emitted X rays as its dominant form of radiation. The announcement of the AS and E discovery was made in August 1962 at a symposium at Stanford University. The curiosity of the scientific world had been raised—but confirmation of this startling revelation was needed. And were there other X-ray sources?

The AS and E scientists used their remaining two Aerobee launches to confirm their results. Gone now was the interest in lunar X rays. The first reflight, on October 12, 1962, detected a new X-ray source (near the Crab Nebula); the second reflight, on June 10, 1963, detected yet another new source, while providing additional data on the bright source near the galactic center. The existence of a new class of celestial X-ray emitters was beyond dispute. X-ray astronomy was heading for the big time.

Friedman and his colleagues at NRL must have been bitterly disappointed that, after all their pioneering work in X-ray technology and a decade of experience in rocket research, others had grabbed the big prize. Friedman had been launching nighttime rockets to look for extrasolar X-ray sources since 1956, and it would surely have been just a matter of time before one scanned past a bright source. However, he was quick to put his disappointment behind him. Friedman had been joined at this time by a young researcher, Stuart Bowyer. Bowyer had developed an X-ray detector 10 times more sensitive than anything previously flown, and collimated so as to give reasonably accurate positional information. With this detector, surely the NRL group would outgun their rivals. An already scheduled rocket experiment was diverted to the task of using the new detector to confirm the AS and E discovery. Launched in late April 1963, the NRL experiment not only confirmed the AS and E detection but positioned the source with some accuracy. It was in the constellation of Scorpius and was christened Scorpius X-1 (the first X-ray source discovered in Scorpius), usually abbreviated to Sco X-1. The NRL detector also scanned across the Crab Nebula, revealing it to be an X-ray source with intensity about 15 percent that of Sco X-1. The experiment also confirmed the presence of an isotropic background flux over the sky. Just six months old, X-ray astronomy had already revealed three different forms of celestial phenomena—X-ray "stars" like Sco X-1 (of uncertain nature), supernova remnants (the Crab Nebula, a predicted source of X rays), and the background radiation (of unknown origin). Confirmation of the AS and E result by the much-respected NRL team meant final acceptance of the new discipline by even the most cautious of observers. The media were now, belatedly, also being caught up in the excitement: *Time, Scientific American*, the *New York Times*, and others all featured the spectacular and unexpected results. X-ray astronomy was here to stay.

The new rocket discoveries obviously had to be taken into account in the planning of future space missions. NASA could no longer place an exploratory X-ray astronomy mission as a low priority. In April 1964, Giacconi and his colleagues submitted to NASA a detailed proposal for such an exploratory mission, as one of NASA's series of small Explorer satellites. (Six months earlier they had presented a draft outline of a 10-year program for X-ray astronomy.) NASA's new enthusiasm for X-ray astronomy was matched by congressional approval in 1965, with funding commencing in 1966. An even more ambitious series of X-ray missions was already on the drawing board—the High Energy Astronomical Observatories (HEAO). Such was the rapid growth in the stature of X-ray astronomy since the discovery of Sco X-1.

In the few years following the AS and E discovery, numerous rocket flights produced data of increasing quality on an expanding catalog of X-ray sources. By 1966, 30 objects had been identified, including the first extragalactic X-ray source (a giant elliptical galaxy called M87, discovered by the NRL group). Much of the pioneering work was undertaken by the Giacconi and Friedman teams, but other research groups (in the United States, the United Kingdom, and elsewhere) were being attracted to the exciting new discipline. Particularly noteworthy was the increase in the number of young astronomers being attracted away from traditional areas of astronomical research and into X-ray astronomy.

Discovering new X-ray sources was proving a reasonably simple task in the early 1960s. But understanding them was proving rather more challenging. What physical processes could possibly explain the prodigious X-ray production rates being discovered? For example, the Crab Nebula was generating X rays at a rate thousands of times greater than the sun was generating energy over the entire electromagnetic spectrum. New models for astrophysical energy generation were clearly needed. Indeed, some even suggested that new laws of physics would be required.

One elegant rocket experiment was devised to elucidate the nature of the Crab Nebula X-ray source. Was the emission coming from the extended nebula, or from a central star? Friedman had learned that the Crab Nebula would be eclipsed by the moon on July 7, 1964, a once-in-a-decade occurrence. The passage of the moon across the nebula could reveal the extent of the source, since an abrupt disappearance of X rays at the time of eclipse would show that it was a star, whereas a gradual variation would show the source to be extended. The experiment was performed successfully and proved that the Crab Nebula source was extended—not the result Friedman himself had predicted, but an important result in the evolving knowledge of the nature of the celestial X-ray sources. (Actually, Friedman was right. Later it would be shown that there is an X-ray star in the Crab Nebula, the pulsar, as well as an extended X-ray source.)

An equally ingenious rocket experiment was performed on March 6, 1966, by MIT scientists working with the AS and E group. (The AS and E and NRL teams each seemed to have little trouble countering the successes of their rivals; they continued to dominate the field, as each strove for ascendancy.) The MIT/AS and E experiment used a novel technique called a rotation-modulation collimator to obtain a dramatically improved positional estimate of Sco X-1, which would make the identification of the optical star possible. The rotation-modulation collimator had been developed by a Japanese professor visiting MIT, Minoru Oda. The launch of the Aerobee rocket was faultless, and excellent data were obtained allowing an accurate positioning of Sco X-1. The AS and E group had made an exclusive agreement with Alan San-dage of the Mount Palomar Observatory to provide him with any accurate determinations of X-ray positions they obtained, so that he could use the 200-inch telescope on Mount Palomar to secure the optical identifications; the results were to be published jointly. (An optical identification of a star producing X rays helps elucidate its nature.) Unfortunately, the cozy arrangement between AS and E and Palomar had not been made known to Oda. He alerted his colleagues back at the University of Tokyo to the new position, and using a 74-inch telescope they identified Sco X-1 with a blue star of intermediate brightness—the first optical identification of an X-ray star. The Palomar observers, understandably aggrieved, got to confirm the result a week later! The Sco X-1 optical identifica-tion confirmed that stars existed emitting approximately 1,000 times more power in X rays than at visible wavelengths, in dra-matic contrast to the sun. Objects like Sco X-1 could not have been foreseen from optical observations.

Intensive optical observations of the blue star would obviously be important in understanding the nature of Sco X-1 and the origin of the X-ray emission. The star looked suspiciously like the stellar remnant of an ancient nova explosion. This was a major clue, since novae are believed to be produced in binary systems. Were X-ray "stars" binary objects? As early as 1964, some theoreticians had speculated that this might be so—that if a compact star (for example, a white dwarf) orbited a normal star, then matter ejected by the large star would be attracted by gravity to the surface of the compact star, where it could be heated to the extreme temperatures required to produce X rays. The discovery of the optical counter-part of Sco X-1 reopened the debate on the binary-star model for X-ray sources. But more X-ray data were needed. And it was diffi-cult to obtain the necessary quality and quantity of data using rocket experiments because of their limited duration. One needed to place experiments in orbit on satellites, so as to get months or even years of data, rather than a scant few minutes per rocket launch. Beginning in 1966, the AS and E group terminated their rocket program to concentrate on the development for NASA of instrumentation for the first satellite dedicated exclusively to X-ray astronomy.

When Giacconi had first proposed to NASA in 1963 an X-ray satellite to produce a catalog of new sources (and estimate the positions, intensity, and spectra), only two X-ray sources had been definitely detected (Sco X-1 and the Crab Nebula). By the time the first satellite dedicated to X-ray astronomy was launched, in late 1970, over 30 had been discovered. By mission's end, 27 months later, more than 300 were known!

One of the class of small, low-budget Explorer missions, the project was known by NASA as the *Small Astronomical Satellite–1* *(SAS-1)*. The instrumentation designed by AS and E was conventional, based on the counter technology developed and proven on rocket experiments, rather than the X-ray-telescope concept originally invoked by Giacconi. In fact, the payload weighed a mere 64 kilograms, not much more than many suitcase-size rocket payloads. After four years of development, the satellite was launched by a Scout rocket from a modified oil platform off the coast of Kenya on December 12, 1970. This unusual launch site was chosen so as to place the satellite in an orbit around the equator under the earth's dangerous radiation belts. Once in orbit, the satellite was named *Uhuru*, from the Swahili word for "freedom," since December 12 was Kenya's Independence Day.

Uhuru was able to make a variety of measurements that would have been difficult, or impossible, from rockets. First, since the satellite was slowly spinning, its detectors scanned many times over the same part of sky; such repeated observations enabled it to detect sources some 10 times fainter than those ever detected from rockets. (Hence the 300 new sources discovered by *Uhuru*!) Second, repeated observations of an object over an extended period made it possible to study how its intensity varied with time. Finally, repeated scans of a source from varying directions enabled positions to be determined with reasonable accuracy.

Probably the most significant discovery by *Uhuru* was that many of the X-ray sources within the Milky Way were, indeed, binary systems. The first such success resulted from *Uhuru* observing a source in Centaurus, Cen X-3, between January and May 1971, early in the mission. The intensity was found to vary rapidly, every 4.8 seconds, suggesting that the X rays were coming from a collapsed, rapidly rotating object (probably a neutron star). A longer periodicity of 2.087 days was also apparent, suggestive of a binary star where the compact object is eclipsed by a larger companion. The identification of the corresponding optical star (the larger companion), exhibiting the same periods, confirmed the binary identification. If one X-ray source was definitely an X-ray binary,

An eclipsing binary. X rays originating from the accretion disc around the compact object in a binary system are eclipsed by the larger companion star.

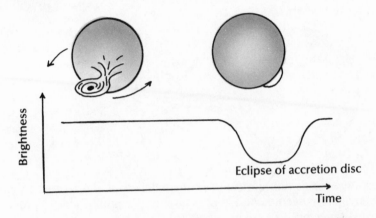

Eclipse of accretion disc

Brightness

Time

presumably some (perhaps the majority) of the other X-ray sources in our galaxy might be also? In late 1971, the AS and E team found that Hercules X-1 (Her X-1) displayed periodicities of 1.24 seconds and 1.7 days—another definite binary catch. Others followed, enabling theoreticians to develop a plausible model for the variable X-ray objects. These were envisaged as close binary systems, in which a compact object (presumably a white dwarf, or a neutron star formed in an earlier supernova explosion) is in orbit around a normal star. Transfer of material from the normal star occurs at a point in its evolution when it expands so that its outer layer comes under the gravitational attraction of the compact object. This material does not fall directly to the surface of the compact object, but via a swirling accretion disc where it is heated to the temperatures required for the generation of X rays.

One object received particular attention, Cygnus X-1 (Cyg X-1). Here *Uhuru* showed that the X-ray source flickered on time scales as brief as milliseconds, but without regular pulsations. Once an optical identification was achieved, it was possible to study the nature of the binary system in some detail. The observations implied that the compact object at the heart of the binary system must have a mass about six times that of the sun. But the maximum mass possible for a neutron star is only about three solar masses. Could the compact object in Cygnus X-1 be a black hole? Black holes had

Binary-star model for X-ray sources

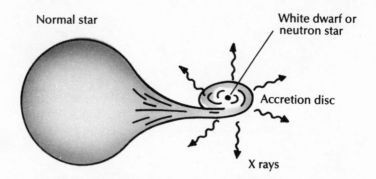

Normal star

White dwarf or
neutron star

Accretion disc

X rays

previously been the playthings of theoreticians and science-fiction writers; it now seemed that X-ray astronomy would be able to prove the existence of these enigmatic celestial objects.

While Giacconi, Friedman, and their colleagues dominated the early years of X-ray astronomy, it would be wrong to overlook the very important contributions from others. A group at the Lockheed Company, under Philip Fisher, were also active pioneers, although dogged by bad luck. They actually had the chance to scoop *Uhuru*, when NASA gave them the opportunity to fly an X-ray detector on the first *Orbiting Astronomical Observatory (OAO)*. However, after launch in April 1966, the spacecraft's power system failed on achieving orbit, and no scientific data were obtained. Stuart Bowyer, initially at NRL with Friedman, started a very successful X-ray astronomy group at the University of California at Berkeley in 1965. His group, and a rival team at the University of Wisconsin under William Kroushaar, concentrated their efforts on the study of the diffuse X-ray background.

The important work done by scientists at the nuclear-weapon laboratories also needs to be acknowledged. At the Lawrence Radiation Laboratory at Livermore, California, a group under Frederick Seward developed rocket-borne detectors to measure X rays emitted from atmospheric nuclear explosions. To monitor Russian compliance with the 1963 Nuclear Test Ban Treaty, instruments were to be launched into space. Rocket test flights were used by Seward's team for X-ray astronomy— a nice piece of opportunism. At the Los Alamos Scientific Laboratory, X-ray detectors were developed to be mounted on the Vela satellites, again with the task of detecting atmospheric nuclear detonations. One of these experiments discovered, in May 1969, the first X-ray nova, Centaurus X-4. As testing of nuclear weapons moved underground, however, the opportunistic X-ray astronomy programs at the nuclear-weapon laboratories were halted.

Plenty was going on elsewhere in the world. In the United Kingdom, X-ray astronomy flourished. There, as in the United States, cosmic X-ray astronomy evolved in research groups who had developed the appropriate technology initially for solar and ionospheric experiments using rocket-borne instruments. Throughout the sixties and early seventies numerous rocket-borne experiments made significant discoveries. Particularly active pioneers were the space research groups of University College, London, under Robert Boyd; and Leicester University, under Ken Pounds; later X-ray astronomy groups evolved at the University of Birmingham and London's Imperial College of Science and Technology. The UCL group, in particular, benefited from the generosity of NASA in flying instruments from foreign institutions—a small UCL X-ray telescope was launched on a NASA spacecraft called *Copernicus* in 1972 and was gathering X-ray data for a full eight years thereafter.

In October 1974 the fifth British scientific satellite, called *Ariel* V, was launched. Dedicated to X-ray astronomy, it carried instruments built by all the United Kingdom X-ray astronomy groups. The scientific returns from *Ariel* V during its five years in orbit exceeded even the most optimistic predictions. It was a mission highlighted by a number of unexpected discoveries. For example, a distinct new class of short-lived transient X-ray sources, which flared brilliantly, was discovered. (An even more bizarre type of extremely brief X-ray phenomenon was discovered later by the Netherlands' ANS spacecraft—the so-called X-ray bursters.) A particular new X-ray source identified by *Ariel* V (called SS433) has proved to be one of the most unusual astronomical objects ever studied—a star system spraying out material at a quarter the speed of light in two finely collimated jets sweeping around the heavens like a giant garden sprinkler. Many of the X-ray sources discovered by *Ariel* V were identified with active galaxies—the enigmatic Seyfert galaxies and quasars.

X-ray astronomy really came of age with the launch of the *High Energy Astrophysics Observatory 2* (*HEAO-2*) on November 13, 1978. (*HEAO-1*, also dedicated to X-ray astronomy, carried instru-

SS 433

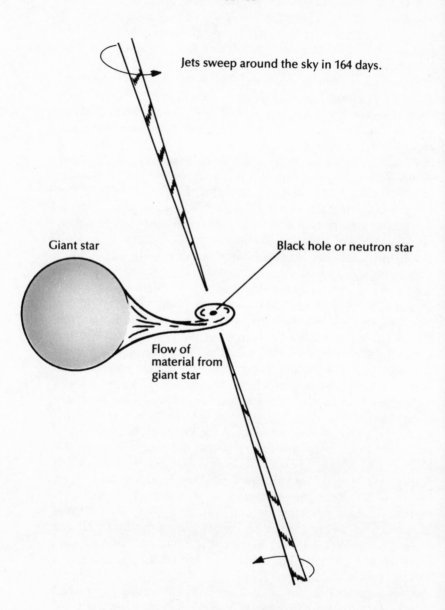

Jets sweep around the sky in 164 days.

Giant star

Black hole or neutron star

Flow of
material from
giant star

ments developed by Friedman, NASA, MIT, and several California groups; although a very successful mission, it was not the epoch-creating mission of its successor.) For Riccardo Giacconi, *HEAO-2* was the fulfillment of a 20-year dream. You will recall that in 1959 Giacconi had conceived the idea of an X-ray telescope using grazing-incidence optics; it was his answer to the problem of capturing sufficient X-ray photons from the then-expected ultra-weak stellar coronal X-ray sources to enable them to be detected. As it turned out, X-ray astronomy had become established using conventional counter technology, because of the unexpected intensity of the binary X-ray sources in particular. Despite the rapid advances being made in X-ray astronomy without the need for telescopes, the AS and E team continued with their long-term (NASA-sponsored) development program in X-ray optics. The advantage of a focusing X-ray optics system is that true images can be obtained. At each stage of the development program, various prototype telescopes could be proven in solar studies. In 1963, the AS and E group obtained the first true X-ray picture of the sun, with a resolution of 1 arc minute; that is, details as fine as 1 arc minute in diameter could be distinguished (there are 60 arc minutes in 1 degree and 60 arc seconds in 1 arc minute). Within a few years the quality of their telescope had improved to a resolution of 5 arc seconds (approaching the resolution obtainable with ground-based optical telescopes). In 1973 an AS and E X-ray solar telescope was flown on the manned *Skylab* mission, when astronauts obtained many thousands of high-quality X-ray images of the sun, which were to enable major advances in our understanding of the physical processes in the solar corona and solar flares. The technology of grazing-incidence X-ray telescopes was now sufficiently advanced for NASA to agree to fly the first large X-ray telescope for celestial studies on the *HEAO-2*. Once in orbit it was christened the *Einstein Observatory*, in recognition of the centenary of the birth of the greatest scientist of modern times. It was one of the most sophisticated spacecraft ever constructed and could point to a desired position in the sky with high precision.

The *Einstein Observatory* X-ray telescope consisted of four nested paraboloids and four nested hyperboloids, with an outer diameter of 58 centimeters. This provided astronomers for the first time with a telescope whose sensitivity to X rays matched the sensitivity of instruments operated on the ground for optical and radio observations. Giacconi proudly claimed that his telescope represented as great an advance in sensitivity over the early X-ray detectors carried above the atmosphere by rockets in 1962 as the Mount Palomar 200-inch telescope represented over Galileo's first astronomical telescope of 1609. In both cases the increase in sensitivity was roughly a millionfold. The advances that had taken optical astronomy over three centuries had been achieved by X-ray astronomy in less than three decades—such has been the accelerating pace of technical achievement.

Instrumentation for the *Einstein Observatory* involved a consortium of several institutions, with the scientific program under Giacconi's direction. In addition to AS and E, groups from MIT, Columbia University, and NASA's Goddard Space Flight Center were involved. Giacconi's group from AS and E had in fact moved to the Center for Astrophysics (CFA), in Cambridge, Massachusetts, in 1973, and CFA would be the center for scientific operations during the mission. Four instruments were available behind the telescope, mounted on a turntable so that they could be rotated to the focus of the telescope as required. Two instruments were specifically for producing X-ray images (one with a large field of view of 1 degree but modest positional resolution of 1 arc minute, the second with a smaller field of view of just 20 arc minutes but high resolution of 4 arc seconds); the other two instruments were to obtain X-ray spectra. Data from the spacecraft were transmitted to NASA ground stations, then relayed to CFA, where advanced data-processing facilities were available. NASA generously made observation time on the *Einstein Observatory* available to guest astronomers from around the world, although the majority of observation time was reserved for members of the scientific consortium who built the instruments and provided the data-analysis systems.

The *Einstein* mission was certainly one of the most successful space projects ever; it succeeded beyond all expectations, recording at X-ray wavelengths every major class of astronomical object. There was no field of cosmic astronomy that did not require significant revision following *Einstein*'s flight. A book could (and should) be written on the major achievements of the *Einstein Observatory*; here we must limit ourselves to a few highlights.

The *Einstein Observatory* revealed that the coronae of normal stars emit far more X-rays than expected from comparison with the sun. Before *Einstein*, the only X-ray "stars" discovered (other than the sun) had been binary systems with intense emission. But now normal stars were being found—not just hot young stars, but also cool stars. Indeed the most surprising results came from the so-called cool stars, ones older than the sun. Whereas a mere 1-millionth of the sun's total radiated power is in X rays, some cool stars were discovered where X rays represented a tenth of the radiated power. It seems that the sun, the most-studied star on which so many of our ideas about stellar phenomena are based, is abnormally faint in X rays. The *Einstein Observatory* disclosed that strong coronal X-ray emission is the norm, rather than the exception, for stars. Classical theories of stellar evolution and energy transport from stars to their coronae just could not explain the new observations.

The vast majority of the 400 X-ray sources known before the *Einstein* mission were thought to be binary systems, with X rays arising from mass transfer from one star to a compact companion (a white dwarf, a neutron star, or a black hole). The *Einstein* mission discovered many hundreds more such X-ray binaries, of a variety of types, with a positional accuracy such that the corresponding optical stars could be identified. Hundreds more extragalactic X-ray sources were found, mainly active galaxies. Within nearby galaxies, such as the Magellanic Clouds and the Great Nebula in Andromeda, individual X-ray sources were identified (over 80 in Andromeda alone), all of comparable intrinsic intensity to the brightest X-ray sources in the Milky Way.

Some of the most spectacular images from *Einstein* were of supernova remnants. Pictured for the first time were the intricate hot filaments—and in some cases, the cooling neutron star at the site of the supernova explosion. A quite remarkable image was of the jets of SS433, burgeoning out into the supernova remnant surrounding it. Spectral observations of supernova remnants revealed that not only was heated interstellar material being observed, but dense knots of ejecta from the star that had exploded were also seen. Comparisons of the high-quality X-ray data from the *Einstein Observatory*, with ground-based optical and radio observations, will keep supernova experts occupied for a long time. Now they have the information they need to study how X-ray supernova remnants evolve; how material blasted out from the exploding star mixes with the surrounding interstellar medium, heating it to high temperatures; how the interstellar medium is enriched both by certain elements fused in the star that exploded and by heavy elements created in the extreme conditions of the supernova outburst; how the stellar remnant (the neutron star) evolves and continues to transmit energy to the expanding remnant; etc.

Uhuru had discovered that the space within clusters of galaxies was pervaded by hot gas at millions of degrees and radiating X rays. The *Einstein Observatory* showed that clusters of galaxies can be characterized by this X-ray emission. In some clusters the X-ray emission is strongly concentrated in the center of the cluster, while in others it is randomly distributed in clumps. Cosmologists must try to find out what it is about the evolution of clusters of galaxies that determines such varied characteristics for the intergalactic gas. The X-ray data provides a more direct way of estimating the total mass of material in a cluster than can be achieved by optical data alone; it might therefore eventually make a significant contribution to solving the missing-mass mystery.

Before the *Einstein* mission, X rays had been detected from only the three nearest quasars. Every previously known quasar (discovered by radio and optical techniques) looked at by *Einstein* was found to emit X rays. Indeed, in many of the 4,000 fields looked at during the mission, X-ray sources were found that were subsequently identified by optical techniques as quasars but that were weak in radio emission (the so-called radio quiet quasars). The most widely accepted candidate for the central powerhouse of a quasar is a giant black hole, millions of times more massive than the sun, at the nucleus of a young galaxy. Infalling stars are torn apart and swallowed up by this gargantuan monster with an insatiable appetite, releasing vast amounts of energy in the process. X rays are expected to be formed nearer to the center of the quasar than is radiation at other wavelengths; thus they probe closer to the heart of the system. The *Einstein* observations verified this, detecting variations in the X-ray output of quasars measured on time scales as short as hours. Since no object can coordinate its activity on its remote side with that on its near side in less time than it takes light to travel across it, a change of intensity over a period of a few hours indicates that the X-ray emission is coming from a region of a few light-hours in diameter (a diameter similar to that of the solar system); by contrast, the optical and radio emissions come from regions tens of light-days or light-years in diameter. The large number of quasars discovered by *Einstein* has raised the possibility that the background X radiation could be due to the summed contribution of billions of individual quasars, too faint to be resolved, rather than truly diffuse emission filling all space.

In 1980, the attitude-control system that enabled the *Einstein Observatory* to point anywhere in the sky and hold that attitude accurately for extended periods, failed catastrophically. The reason for the sudden loss of control is unknown. Precious quantities of the fuel for the small attitude-control jets were expended in regaining control of the spacecraft. Thereafter operations had to be limited so as to conserve the small amount of fuel remaining. Much excellent science was done during the few months remaining to it, but eventually control was lost. But few despaired for too long over *Einstein's* premature demise: It had served astronomy gloriously, and the excitement it generated would last for a long time. After the *Einstein* mission, the X-ray universe could never look the same again; astronomy could never be the same again. It had worked miracles, yet had observed a mere 5 percent of the sky. What wonders does the X-ray universe still hold in store?

After the remarkable success of the *Einstein Observatory*, it was perhaps inevitable that any X-ray mission following it would be an anticlimax, and so it proved. The British had planned to follow their very successful *Ariel V* X-ray mission with another small satellite carrying instruments for X-ray astronomy; but *Ariel VI* was burdened from the outset with technical difficulties, including problems with determining exactly where the instruments were pointing. Its contributions to X-ray astronomy can most kindly be described as minimal, although a cosmic-ray experiment on board did give useful results. ESA planned the *EXOSAT* project, their first venture into X-ray astronomy, while *Uhuru* was still in orbit. However, it was so long in the planning and construction that the science originally planned for it was "scooped" by the *Einstein* project. *EXOSAT* performed "useful" X-ray astronomy, rather than the spectacular science of *Einstein*. The Japanese flew two small X-ray satellites and have a third in orbit, again best described as "useful" projects.

If the *Einstein Observatory* observed just 5 percent of the sky with its advanced X-ray telescope, what about the rest? A project called *ROSAT*, conceived by West German scientists but to be jointly funded by West Germany, the United States, and Great Britain, with imaging capability very similar to that of the *Einstein Observatory*, will be launched toward the end of the eighties. *ROSAT* will cover the whole sky in a detailed survey, with a resolution and sensitivity comparable to that of *Einstein*. But what X-ray astronomers *really* want are two major new facilities: first, a larger, more advanced version of the *Einstein Observatory* that could be serviced and upgraded in orbit and that would last two decades or longer; and second, a project that would enable X-ray astronomers to do high-resolution spectroscopy on even faint sources, as their colleagues in optical astronomy are able to do. High-resolution imaging is, of course, important, but the major advances in astrophysics and astrochemistry are most likely to come from spectroscopic observations.

The major, long-term X-ray observatory is being planned by NASA—the *Advanced X-ray Astronomical Facility (AXAF)*. A complementary spectroscopy mission is being planned by ESA— the *High Throughput Spectroscopy (HTS)* mission. Both should be in orbit by the turn of the century, 40 years after the birth of X-ray astronomy. Well, *"life* begins at 40."

Interlude 2 • On the Wings of Mercury

How does a space mission come into being? In the Prologue we claimed that only part of the rationale behind the venture into space has been scientific. The Mercury project, the initial U.S. program to launch man into space, may have been part adventure, part political posturing; the Gemini and Apollo programs were definitely biased toward the latter, since adventure and science alone could never have justified the enormous investment of capital and technical know-how in the moon race. It was the manned space program, however, that compressed into a mere decade what might otherwise have been a century of technical and scientific advancement necessary for the conquest of space. At the height of the Apollo program, NASA's budget, in real terms, was three times that of today. It is unlikely that we will ever again see such a high investment, and as a consequence such a rapid advance of relevant technology, in our efforts to conquer space. Even the Strategic Defense Initiative ("Star Wars") will not attract the investment in space technology in such a short time as the moon program did.

Astronomy was able to take to the skies on the "wings of Mercury." Without the adventure and political elements of space, astronomers would still be largely earthbound, although it must be emphasized that space astronomy can largely be carried out by robot spacecraft.

So how does an astronomer or space scientist get an instrument, costing tens or perhaps hundreds of millions of hard-earned taxpayers' dollars, launched into space? The first step is for an individual scientist, or group of scientists, to identify a need for a particular type of observation and put forward a proposal as to how such observations could be made. Advisory panels of experts often

57

give advice to the space agencies on the types of experiments that should be undertaken. The leading scientist on any mission proposal is called the principal investigator, or PI; his collaborators are the co-investigators, or Co-Is. A PI will attempt to attract to his collaboration the most prestigious group of Co-Is possible, to give his proposal the necessary stature in the highly competitive world of space research.

Proposals to fly instruments are often solicited by the space agencies, but they may arise on an ad hoc basis. Because of the high cost of most space projects, with few exceptions they can be undertaken only through the space agencies. They are usually subjected to some form of scientific peer assessment before undergoing detailed technical scrutiny. Such is the complexity of most space missions that this process alone might take a year or more. (Many space scientists would claim that lengthy time scales are more often determined by the unwieldy bureaucracy of the space agencies than by any technical and planning difficulties.) If the scientific case is an outstanding one, and technical feasibility is proved, a competitive selection then has to be made among projects competing for the scarce resources of the various space agencies. The efforts expended in this competitive selection process often appear to know no bounds, and one wonders how science could become so political; so often it all ends in disappointment for scientists who may have invested many years of their careers in developing new techniques in the laboratory in the hope that they might eventually be tried in space. In space research, it is only the most able (and lucky!) who prosper. Perhaps for this reason, the majority of successful space researchers are hardened, ambitious professionals, active in the rough-and-tumble of astro*politics*, as well as highly creative in astro*science*. Entrepreneurial flair is just as necessary as academic stature for those who want to make the big time in space research.

There are five clearly identifiable components of any space project—the spacecraft, the launch vehicle, the scientific instruments, the ground-control center, and the facilities for scientific analysis. The spacecraft would usually be designed and constructed by industry, by one of the large aerospace companies, or sometimes, for very large projects, by an international consortium of aerospace companies.

Several different models of a spacecraft might be needed to perform particular tasks in the development of the final spacecraft that is to be launched into orbit. The flight spacecraft would normally include a guidance system to point the scientific instruments to a desired direction (there are usually strict limitations on this; for example, sensitive instruments could not be exposed to the sun, moon, or the earth's limb), a power system to provide electrical power to the spacecraft (including solar panels to convert light from the sun into electrical energy stored in a battery), a data-handling system for processing scientific data from the different instruments and monitoring their performance and that of the spacecraft, and a communication system for receiving control signals from the ground and returning scientific data.

The scientific instruments might be constructed by industry, but they are often built in universities or scientific establishments. Before being launched into orbit, the various instruments and spacecraft systems must be rigorously tested to ensure that they will survive the harsh space environment. For example, the spacecraft might be subjected to temperature extremes from near absolute zero to several hundreds of degrees; the near vacuum of space and the lack of gravity present special problems for the operation of moving components; materials give off gases that might then condense on sensitive surfaces; particle radiation from the sun can damage sensitive electronic circuits; etc.

Reliability is essential in a spacecraft, and this inevitably means extremely careful testing, built-in redundancy of major components, and exceptional levels of quality control in production of the spacecraft. All these factors contribute to the high cost of a space mission; there is added complexity where astronauts are involved since human safety demands even greater control. However, despite all the precautions, testing, and backup systems, things do sometimes go tragically wrong.

After the launch of a scientific spacecraft, a ground station has responsibility for planning the operations of the spacecraft, sending it control signals, receiving back scientific data, checking the health of the spacecraft, preanalyzing scientific data and distributing it to interested scientists, etc. Some space-astronomy satellites are now operated very much like a ground-based observatory; astronomers visit the ground station during the time their observations are being made, check that the spacecraft is pointed toward the correct position in the sky, observe the data being displayed as it is received from the spacecraft, and arrange for adjustments to instruments, just as they do with a ground-based

Contributors to a space mission

Prelaunch

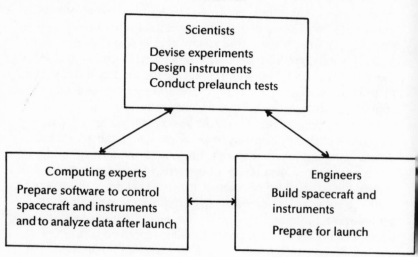

- -

Postlaunch

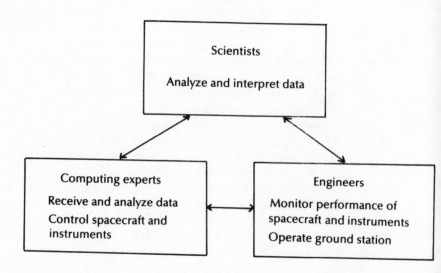

telescope—except that the telescopes they are controlling may be thousands of kilometers away in space. Data can be returned to Earth in real time (that is, as it is being acquired), or can be stored on board on a tape recorder or some other data-storage device, to be sent back to Earth later under appropriate command. A satellite ground control center can be a very exciting place to be, especially during critical times of a mission—when instruments are switched on for the first time, when a delicate adjustment is to be performed on the spacecraft, or when a particular scientific experiment is to be performed. Many of the people present may have invested a large part of their working careers in this particular space project, so it is really not too surprising that tension can be high. Space research has a language all its own—a mixture of acronyms, abbreviations, slang, and catch phrases. A visitor to a space control center would be able to sense the excitement but would be unlikely to understand the exchanges.

The orbit chosen for a satellite depends on its objectives. In a geostationary orbit, a satellite at 36,000 kilometers above the equator has an orbital period identical to that of the earth's rotation; thus it appears to hover above the same position on the earth's surface. To reach geostationary orbit, satellites are launched into an elliptical transfer orbit by an unmanned launcher (such as the European Arianne rocket), with the satellite's own motor being used to position it in its final circular geostationary orbit. For launches from a space shuttle, an upper-stage booster rocket is required to take a satellite destined for geostationary orbit from the shuttle's altitude (about 400 kilometers). The majority of scientific satellites are, in fact, placed in low Earth orbit—at an altitude of, say, 1,000 kilometers—and circle the globe once every 100 minutes or so. The inclination of the orbit with respect to the equatorial plane can be selected depending on the scientific objectives of the mission although there are constraints from various launch sites.

The advent of the shuttle (more correctly, the Space Transportation System, or STS) has brought a new dimension to the design of scientific satellites. Now recovery or refurbishment in orbit is one of the factors that can be planned into space missions. Until the tragic loss of the *Challenger* on January 28, 1986, it seemed that just about anything was possible from the shuttle; it seemed to embody the can-do spirit of U.S. space engineers and scientists. Dead satellites could be reactivated in space; instruments

The geostationary orbit. A satellite is first boosted into a transfer orbit, then into geostationary orbit by firing the spacecraft motor at point *L*.

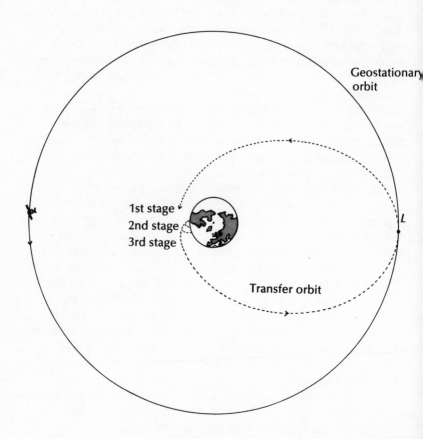

could be placed in orbit on one mission and recovered on the next; experiments could be assembled in space; satellites that failed to achieve the required orbits could be rescued. But the spirit of *Challenger* lives on. In President Ronald Reagan's words, "The future does not belong to the fainthearted; it belongs to the brave."

Thus the scope of astronomical research from space calls on the skills of a host of research disciplines: for example, those of the engineers who design and build the rockets, spacecraft, and instruments and who extend engineering techniques to new bounds of precision and reliability; those of the designers and operators of ground stations who use highly sophisticated computers to control the spacecraft and to process the information they acquire; and those of the astronomers, physicists, and mathematicians who interpret the astronomical data in terms of known natural processes. Finally, for satellites launched, repaired, or recovered by the shuttle, or for instruments operated from the shuttle, there is the bravery and commitment of the men and women who venture across the new frontier. Those involved will tell you that space is enormously exciting. Few of them would wish to change their lot, despite the demands and the frustrations. For the professional, space research is not merely an occupation; it is an addiction.

—— 3 ——
THE REALM OF HEPHAESTUS

INFRARED LIGHT IS FAMILIAR TO US AS HEAT RADIATION. Although our eyes do not see infrared radiation, our bodies can sense it; stand close to a fire and you can feel the heat being radiated from it. The only celestial furnace we can sense directly, however, is the sun. To detect infrared radiation from other objects in the cosmos, very sensitive detectors are needed. Technology must give us "infrared eyes" to explore the realm of Hephaestus, god of fire.

The existence of invisible radiation, at wavelengths beyond the red, was demonstrated for the first time in 1800 by William Herschel. A spectrum of the sun's radiation was produced using a simple prism. In the region of the spectrum beyond the red, where nothing could be seen, Herschel held a thermometer; it showed an increase in temperature, recording the heat radiation from the sun at wavelengths greater than that of visible red light. This was the first simple astronomical experiment ever performed in any radiation outside visible light. Half a century later, infrared radiation was detected from the moon, and in the first few decades of this century infrared observations of some of the planets and a few bright stars were made. (In the case of the moon and planets, the infrared light is the reradiation of energy received from the sun.) Despite these few simple experiments, infrared astronomy could hardly be said to have emerged as a serious astronomical discipline, nor could it have been expected to be a significant branch of astronomy, until technology could come to its aid.

Infrared radiation extends from wavelengths of about a micron (0.001 millimeters) to hundreds of microns, beyond which lies the microwave region. The difficulties in carrying out infrared astronomy are manifold. First, most of the infrared light from cosmic objects is heavily absorbed by certain molecules in the earth's atmosphere, especially molecules of carbon dioxide and water vapor. From sea level, we can detect some infrared wavelengths between about 1 and 3 microns (the so-called near-infrared region), but little else. If one can get to a high mountaintop in a dry climate, other infrared "windows" (that is, spectral gaps in the atmospheric opacity through which we can view the cosmos) are usable, near 5, 10, and 20 microns. The earth's atmosphere itself radiates in the infrared, with wavelengths characteristic of the molecules of air— the same wavelengths at which atmospheric absorption is most acute. Even from mountaintops, the faint infrared signals from distant celestial sources are competing with the confusing radiation from the atmosphere. (From the air, it would be easy to sight a sapling in a desert, but more difficult to find it in a forest.) Not only that, any telescope and detector system used will itself emit infrared radiation by virtue of being warm, and this problem must be dealt with by cooling the telescope and detector system. No wonder infrared astronomy made slow progress in moving from its first tentative pioneering steps to the point today where it is one of the most exciting and rewarding of astronomical disciplines.

Many types of astronomical objects and phenomena radiate copiously at infrared wavelengths; most notably, objects made up of relatively cool, solid material. The temperatures involved for these objects may, in fact, be many hundreds of degrees (that is, extremely hot on a human scale but cold on a cosmic scale). As the temperature of astronomical objects increases to thousands of degrees, most of the energy is radiated at visible and ultraviolet wavelengths. In the infrared, the systems are relatively cool. At a temperature of 500 degrees Celsius, an object radiates most strongly in the *near* infrared, at a wavelength of just a few microns; at a temperature of − 250 degrees Celsius (close to the lowest possible temperature of − 273 degrees) an object radiates most strongly in the *far* infrared, at several hundred microns. (The human body, at 37 degrees Celsius, radiates most strongly at about 10 microns; so does the earth!)

The first major survey of the infrared sky was undertaken in the 1960s, by Gerry Neugebauer and Bob Leighton of Cal Tech, using a ground-based telescope. The near-infrared atmospheric window at 2 microns was used, and almost 6,000 sources were discovered. To start to compete with the problems caused by the atmosphere, cooled infrared telescopes were carried aloft on high-altitude balloons and high-flying aircraft. Astronomy with balloons has met with marginal success; a few important discoveries have been made, but the frustrations and disappointments of astronomy from balloons have certainly outnumbered the successes. Far more successful for infrared astronomy have been observations from high-flying aircraft. Most noted of these has been the *Kuiper Airborne Observatory*, a 1-meter-diameter telescope flown on a C141 transport aircraft operated by NASA. During flight, the aircraft's autopilot system is connected to the computer which keeps the telescope pointing at the star or star system under investigation: The telescope flies the plane! But even from aircraft altitudes, there are still residual atmospheric problems. Ideally, one needs to get right above the atmosphere, out into space. Of course, important infrared astronomy can be done through certain atmospheric windows from high mountaintops and from aircraft, but the advantages of getting above the atmosphere are enormous. Infrared instruments were put on rockets and achieved certain discoveries. But to be really successful, you need to get a cooled telescope out into space, on an orbiting satellite.

Plans to put an infrared telescope in space started in earnest in 1974. It was to become known as the *Infrared Astronomical Satellite* (IRAS), a joint project between the United States, the Netherlands, and the United Kingdom. One of the most heartening aspects of space research over the years has been the extent to which nations have collaborated on joint projects. Certainly neither the Netherlands nor the United Kingdom could have hoped to sponsor a mission of the cost and complexity of IRAS on a purely national basis, and the United States has always been keen to use space and the resources of NASA as a component of its foreign policy. At the center of IRAS planning from the outset was Cal Tech's Gerry Neugebauer. One must always acknowledge the extensive involvement of a large team of scientists, engineers, and technicians in any space mission, but so often a single individual stands out at the center of scientific and political activity. Just as Giacconi had been "Mr. *Einstein*," Neugebauer would prove to be "Mr. *IRAS*."

The Netherlands Agency for Aerospace Programs (NIVR) and NASA had independently started studies in the early 1970s for a cooled infrared telescope in space. Shortly after they decided to join forces in 1974, the United Kingdom became the third member of the *IRAS* club. NASA would have the largest share of the project—to build the telescope, the detectors, and the cryogenic system that would cool it to very low temperatures so that there would be no confusing heat radiation from the telescope itself. Responsibility for managing the project and completing final analysis of the survey data from *IRAS* was given to Cal Tech's Jet Propulsion Laboratory at Pasadena, California. The Netherlands undertook the task of building the remaining parts of the spacecraft —the power system, the on-board computers, and the system for pointing the telescope. The United Kingdom was to build a ground station at the Rutherford Appleton Laboratory in Oxfordshire to receive data from the satellite and transmit commands to it. It took eight years from the commencement of detailed planning in 1974 until launch on January 25, 1983, from the Vandenberg Air Force Base in California—about par for the course for a major space project.

IRAS had as its main goal a discovery survey of the whole of the infrared sky in four discrete wavelength bands centered on 12, 25, 60, and 100 microns. In each of its 300 days in operation, *IRAS* would discover more infrared sources than all those known before its launch!

The *IRAS* reflecting telescope was of 60-centimeter aperture, enclosed (apart from, obviously, the entrance aperture) by an insulated cooling vessel containing about 500 liters of liquid helium. This held the temperature of the telescope system to just a few degrees above absolute zero (-273 degrees Celsius), minimizing the problem of residual heat radiated from the telescope itself. So cooled, *IRAS* was so sensitive that it could have detected, from London, the heat from a baseball in Yankee Stadium in New York. In orbit the coolant slowly evaporated away, so that it was totally expended in 300 days, after which the telescope and detectors warmed up and the system lost its sensitivity to infrared radiation.

The extreme sensitivity of the *IRAS* telescope and detectors (which could pick up a speck of dust at several kilometers) itself produced problems. Spurious signals would be expected from dust and debris in the vicinity of the spacecraft. To sift the wanted signals from cosmic sources from the unwanted signals from local debris, only those signals that could be confirmed by repeated observations over time were cataloged as true cosmic infrared sources.

The main survey instrument comprised eight staggered rows of detectors, there being two rows for each of the four wavelength ranges surveyed. The telescope swept over the sky in a direction at

Detectors in the focal plane of the *IRAS* telescope

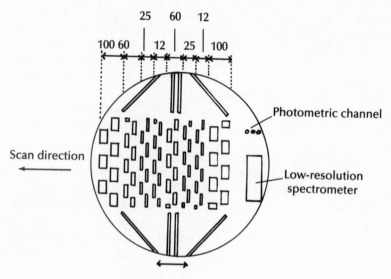

Visible-light star sensors

right angles to the rows of detectors, so that an infrared source would sweep over the first row at a particular wavelength, then a few seconds later over the second row: Detection in both rows meant that a source was "seconds confirmed" (that is, its reality was confirmed over a timescale of seconds). A source detected on two consecutive orbits was then said to be "hours confirmed." Seconds and hours confirmation certainly sorted out true cosmic sources from unwanted detections of dust and debris (including the large amount of man-made junk now orbiting in space). Finally, reexamination of the same areas of the sky sometimes allowed "months confirmation." By these various means, the *IRAS* survey achieved an extremely high standard of reliability and completeness. Ninety-five percent of the sky was surveyed with at least hours-confirmed detections.

About 60 percent of the observing time on *IRAS* was used on the all-sky survey. The rest of the time was used for pointed observations of sources of particular interest. In addition to the survey detectors, there were two other instruments onboard. The first was a low-resolution spectrometer able to record infrared spectra of bright sources; the second was a detector for mapping selected sources with higher spatial resolution than could be achieved with the survey detectors.

By any measure (even the high standards of *Uhuru* or *Einstein*) the *IRAS* mission was an outstanding success. The infrared represented one of the final vistas for astronomy. We had mapped the heavens at ultraviolet and X-ray wavelengths from space. Only a few premature glimpses of the infrared horizon had been obtained; but now *IRAS* had brought it all sharply into focus. And what a panorama had been revealed! Astronomers viewed with awe this new vision of the cosmos, like a child, blind since birth, suddenly given the gift of sight.

The findings of *IRAS* bear on all areas of astronomical research, from comets, asteroids, and planets in the solar system to distant quasars and protogalaxies. As *Uhuru* had revealed in X rays the violent universe of stellar explosions, black holes, and galaxies in upheaval, *IRAS* had revealed in infrared radiation the serene universe, of planets, stars, and galaxies.

Matter in the solar system tends to reradiate in infrared light most of the energy it receives from the sun. The cloud of dust in the ecliptic plane (the plane of the sky in which the planets orbit) is prominent in the infrared; this is the dust responsible for the zodiacal light. This dust may be the debris from colliding asteroids or old comets; it is believed to be made up principally of iron and magnesium silicates (like rocks on Earth), with particle sizes from just a few microns to sand-size specks. The detailed structure of this zodiacal infrared emission was revealed for the first time by *IRAS* in the short wavelength bands. In addition to the dense ring in the ecliptic plane, there are outlying bands on either side of the principal ring. The additional bands are probably part of a single ring, inclined at about 10 degrees to the principal ring. What might be the origin of this second ring? One interesting possibility is that it is the debris from the collision of an asteroid and a comet.

At longer wavelengths, *IRAS* discovered an intriguing additional component to the infrared background. Faint, wispy "clouds," referred to as infrared cirrus, engulf the celestial sphere. Analysis revealed that the infrared cirrus must lie far out in the ultimate extremities of the solar system (far beyond the orbit of Pluto). Indeed, it may be associated with the Oort Cloud (named after the famous Dutch astronomer Jan Oort). The Oort Cloud is believed to be the icy home of debris from the nascent solar system that failed to accumulate into planets. It is the likely source of the comets. The passage of a nearby star is thought to deflect some of this debris in toward the sun; an isolated chunk of icy debris is then witnessed as a comet as it sweeps past the sun and volatile gases boil from its surface. (An alternative theory for the origin of comets is that they are fragments of interstellar debris, captured by the solar system in its passage through the Milky Way.) The standard model for a comet is that of a "dirty snowball," comprising dust and ice. But what a snowball! The nucleus of a comet is believed to be the size of Mount Everest. Gas and dust from the nucleus are then swept back into the characteristic cometary tail by the action of the solar wind and radiation pressure (thus a comet's tail always points away from the sun).

When data from *IRAS* were received at the ground station at the Rutherford Appleton Laboratory (some 700 million bits of image data, equivalent to the complete *Encyclopedia Britannica*, twice each day), it was put through a preliminary computer analysis to look for sources that appeared to have moved between two hours-confirming observations. Now, such sources could be spurious (local debris), or genuine transitory bodies in the solar system such as asteroids and comets. In fact, comets and asteroids were discovered in unexpected numbers. The first *IRAS* comet discovery was on April 26, 1983. Comets are normally named after their discoverers, but none had ever been named after a spacecraft before. In fact the role of two amateur astronomers who sighted the comet shortly after the *IRAS* detection was also acknowledged, and it was named Comet IRAS-Araki-Alcock. On May 11, 1983, Comet IRAS-Araki-Alcock passed within 3 million kilometers of the earth, closer than any other comet in the past two centuries. The *IRAS* images showed that the infrared tail of the comet extended to far greater distances than revealed in ground-based optical observations. It seemed that dust was being shed from the comet's nucleus to its extended tail at a rate of several hundred kilograms per second—far faster than had been thought previously. By mission's end, *IRAS* had found five new comets—an unexpectedly high discovery rate.

One of the most unexpected *IRAS* discoveries was made on October 11, 1983. It was given the rather unglamorous title of 1983 TB. At first it was thought to be just an asteroid. But its orbit was unusual in the extreme. It seems that its path sweeps inward, toward the sun, passing well within the orbit of Mercury and a mere 20 million kilometers above the solar surface. This peculiar trajectory was quickly associated with the so-called Geminid meteorites, which create an annual shower of "shooting stars" in the December night sky. Meteorites are thought to be minute fragments of cometary debris; since the object 1983 TB appears to be the parent body of the Geminid meteorites, it is possible that *IRAS* made the first-ever discovery of the remnant nucleus of a dead comet.

One of the mysteries of solar-system astronomy has been whether there is a tenth planet lying outside the orbit of Pluto. The hypothetical need for an additional planet has been inferred by peculiarities in the motion of the outer planets, where gravity doesn't seem to behave itself. This same reasoning, in fact, led to the discovery of Pluto. In the early decades of this century, astronomers searched for an outer planet beyond Neptune, since it seemed the paths of the outer planets were being perturbed by another, invisible, body. In 1929, the required planet was duly found and named Pluto. But Pluto appeared to be too small to explain the perturbations of the orbits of Neptune and Uranus. So, was there a Planet X beyond Pluto? If anything was going to discover the missing planet, it was felt *IRAS* could. Well, maybe. Perhaps hidden away in the mountain of *IRAS* data is evidence for the existence of Planet X, but it hasn't been found yet.

So much for the planets (known or inferred) of the solar system. An enormously exciting discovery by *IRAS* was evidence for planetary systems forming around other stars. And if planetary systems are a common phenomenon in the cosmos, presumably, are life forms also? Vega is a very bright, young star, about three times the mass of the sun. The ultraviolet and visible spectra of Vega were well studied and well understood, so the likely infrared behavior had been anticipated. What was expected was that at 12 microns the star would be at its brightest in the infrared but that at the longer *IRAS* wavelength bands the intensity would fall off rapidly. But it didn't. There was obviously something else there, other than the star, responsible for the unexpected infrared brightness. Clever detective work on the *IRAS* data indicated that Vega had a ring of gravel-size dust particles surrounding it at a distance comparable to the orbit of Saturn. Vega is a much younger star than the sun, probably just a few hundred million years old, whereas the sun is some 5 billion years old. Perhaps the gravel ring around Vega represents a nascent planetary system in formation. Maybe our solar system went through a similar evolutionary phase before rings condensed to form planets. Evidence was also found by *IRAS* for solid matter orbiting dozens of other stars—again, presumably, planetary systems in formation or being. Of course, *IRAS* didn't have the resolution to actually "see" the gravel rings or planets, but rather was able to infer their existence.

The infrared is a powerful probe of the birthplaces of the stars, and here *IRAS* was truly in its element. One of the most noticeable things about the infrared sky is that the obscuring clouds that hide stars from view at optical wavelengths are found themselves to be radiating in the far infrared, confirming that they are cool dust clouds. Some of the dense dust clouds must have central heat sources to keep them radiating, most probably stars in formation. Star-forming regions are clearly of immense interest to astronomers, and bright infrared sources detected by *IRAS* embedded in dense clouds are thought, indeed, to be stars at their birth. The nascent star itself is not actually seen; rather it is the surrounding cocoon of dust heated by the fledgling to hundreds of degrees. Other infrared "knots" in dust clouds may be dense regions on the point of collapsing to become stars. The infrared observations provide astronomers with their most powerful tool yet for studying the mysteries of stellar birth.

Infrared observations are also important for studying stars at an advanced stage of evolution, especially in the red-giant phase. Release of gas and dust by a red giant results in a shell of what is called circumstellar material that absorbs the star's light (mainly in the visible and ultraviolet) and reradiates it in the infrared. The rate of mass loss from a red giant can be quite spectacular, and it accelerates as the star grows older: Initially material equivalent to the mass of the sun may be lost by a red giant in 100,000 years or so, but eventually that amount of material may be lost in just a few millennia (a mere blink of an eye on cosmic time scales). *IRAS* discovered vast numbers of these highly evolved red giants embedded in circumstellar shells of their own making.

Infrared radiation can probe the very heart of the Milky Way, which is totally obscured from view at visible wavelengths. Actually the center of the Milky Way had been studied prior to *IRAS*, from aircraft and balloon experiments (as well as with detailed radio-astronomy mapping, where obscuration is not a problem). But the *IRAS* infrared images showed much fainter detail than previously recognized. An intriguing feature revealed by *IRAS* are smoky tendrils of enormous scale, extending above and below the nucleus of the Milky Way.

IRAS detected tens of thousands of other galaxies. The brightest infrared source outside the Milky Way is a galaxy called M82. The nucleus of M82 radiates as much energy in the far infrared as the total starlight from the Milky Way. The reason for its extreme infrared brightness is uncertain; one theory is that M82 has collided with a huge intergalactic dust cloud.

IRAS showed a phenomenal range in the infrared brightness of galaxies. In some instances the galaxy is so faint in infrared radiation that it can be entirely explained as the emission from the galaxy's star population. In other cases almost the entire radiation from a galaxy appears to be in the infrared. The overriding factor in the infrared brightness of a galaxy seems to be the quantity of dust present. Thus, elliptical galaxies have a negligible dust content; they are faint in the infrared. By contrast spiral galaxies tend to be rich in dust and bright in the infrared. Where resolution allowed, detailed mapping by *IRAS* confirmed that the infrared emission of spiral galaxies was concentrated in the "dusty" nucleus and dust lanes along the leading edge of the spiral arms.

In those cases where galaxies show extreme infrared brightness, the likely cause is that a galaxy is experiencing a period of exceptionally rapid star formation. In these so-called starburst galaxies, it is estimated that many hundreds of solar masses of interstellar material must be being formed into new stars each year: Such a period of rapid star formation could be only a short-lived phenomenon in galactic evolution (perhaps just a few hundred million years). The hot young stars being formed in a starburst galaxy would heat the interstellar dust (obscuring the stars from view in the visible spectrum) to provide the extreme infrared brightness. Starburst galaxies remain a poorly understood phenomenon. It has been surmised that epochs of rapid star formation may be triggered by collisions of galaxies, and it is an intriguing fact that *IRAS* revealed that the ultrabright infrared galaxies invariably had close companions. Infrared emission was detected by *IRAS* from certain quasars and

Seyfert galaxies; in these cases the intense ultraviolet and X-ray emission from the nucleus heats circumnuclear dust, which then radiates in the infrared.

Although the *IRAS* mission lasted for a mere 300 days (actually longer than its initial life expectancy), the detailed analysis of its data will take astronomers many years to complete. Its impact on astronomy will last for decades. Infrared astronomy may have been a late starter in the space game—but what an impressive opening it has made!

At wavelengths beyond the far infrared lies the microwave region. The importance to astronomy of the microwaves from the cosmos had never been fully appreciated, for it was here that astronomers would detect the faint echo of the creation, in the discovery of the remnant microwave background radiation.

The story of the discovery of the microwave background reads like a replay of Jansky's accidental discovery of the cosmic radio emission. Arno Penzias and Robert Wilson were, like Jansky, from the Bell Telephone Laboratories. In 1965 they were using a sensitive radio antenna built, just a mile from the original site of Jansky's antenna, as part of the communications-satellite program. Just as Jansky had been mystified by his detection of an unexpected radio emission of apparent celestial origin, Penzias and Wilson were equally puzzled by a background microwave radiation that seemed to be coming uniformly from all parts of the sky. They were unaware of a prediction in the same year by Robert Dicke of Princeton University (based on work some 15 years earlier by George Gamow of the University of Colorado) that if the universe had in fact originated in the Big Bang, then some remnant radiation of the holocaust should still be observable. Dicke and his colleagues were preparing to search for the weak remnant radiation when news reached them of its discovery by the Bell engineers. The detection of the faint microwave background radiation was one of the most important discoveries of recent decades; Penzias and Wilson were to be rewarded in 1978 with the Nobel prize.

The microwave radiation appeared to be coming uniformly from all directions with an intensity expected from matter at slightly less than 3 degrees above absolute zero (hence the radiation is sometimes referred to as the "3-degree background"). The form of the radiation was predicted to be that from a so-called black body (a perfect absorber and emitter of radiation), with peak intensity at a wavelength of about 2 millimeters but falling away quite sharply at both longer and shorter wavelengths.

As already explained, the primordial universe was a dense soup of particles and radiation. For hundreds of thousands of years following the Big Bang, the density of material of the universe would have been such that it was essentially opaque to radiation. But then the expanding universe cooled to the point (about 3,000 degrees) where electrons could combine with nuclei to form complete atoms—the epoch of neutralization. From then on, the universe became abruptly transparent to the remnant radiation; now radiation could expand freely, decoupled from the matter in the universe. This is the radiation, initially of a wavelength of about 0.001 millimeters but having been subjected to extreme red shift, that we now observe as the microwave background. At the time of neutralization the universe was a mere 1-billionth of its present volume. The microwave background radiation appears essentially uniform (isotropic) over the sky, at least within the accuracy we are presently able to measure; however, we cannot yet say that at the epoch of matter-radiation decoupling (long before the formation of galaxies) the universe was essentially uniform. More accurate observations are needed.

The atmosphere is almost opaque at wavelengths shorter than about 3 millimeters (again, it is the problem of absorption by air molecules, although dry mountaintop sites do allow observations through certain atmospheric windows at wavelengths down to less than a millimeter). To investigate the true nature of the microwave background, there is only so much that can be achieved from the ground; one really needs to get a cooled detector into space. Experiments were tried from rockets and balloons; although the experiments were enormously difficult, they appeared to confirm black-body radiation with a temperature close to 3 degrees.

But is the microwave background truly isotropic, or could there be small variations in intensity with direction, which could indicate a "lumpy" early universe? (Lumpiness might indicate a structure that led to the first stages of the formation of galaxies.) From the ground it is impossible to separate any such direction dependence intrinsic to the cosmic radiation from effects due to the atmosphere. Again, we need to get into space.

Perhaps the *COBE* (*Cosmic Background Explorer*) will provide all the answers. *COBE* is a NASA satellite to be launched in about

1990 to measure and map the diffuse background radiation from the early universe. It will be looking back in time to the epoch of change when the universe became transparent to radiation, within a mere million years of the Big Bang. However, by understanding this epoch in the evolution of the universe, we may find the answers to a number of questions in cosmology. What was the nature of the Big Bang? Was the explosion turbulent? Was it the same everywhere? How did the galaxies form and cluster?

As on *IRAS*, the instruments on *COBE* will be cooled to an extremely low temperature (within 2 degrees of absolute zero) by the evaporation of liquid helium. The supply of liquid helium should last for about a year, long enough for *COBE* to map the diffuse background radiation over the whole sky. The three instruments on *COBE* will measure the radiation over the wavelength range from 1 micron to 1 centimeter. The first instrument is called the diffuse-microwave radiometer, designed to accurately map the sky at wavelengths of 3.3, 5.7, and 9.6 millimeters. Its principal task will be to determine whether the early universe was equally hot and dense everywhere, that is, is the background really isotropic? The instrument is so sensitive that it will be able to measure any difference in brightness between two points in the sky to within .001 percent of the brightness of the cosmic background radiation —an amazing accuracy given the faintness of the radiation.

The second *COBE* instrument is the far-infrared spectrophotometer, which is designed to measure with extreme precision the spectrum of the background radiation between wavelengths of 0.1 and 10 millimeters. Is the spectrum really that of a black-body emitter? That is, are we really looking at the remnant radiation from the Big Bang fireball? The detector in this instrument is a balometer (an extremely sensitive thermometer), which can measure a power that is only about a hundred-trillionth of a watt. (This is about the power received by a postage stamp in Washington, DC, from a light bulb in New York.) The experiment will be able to measure departures from the predicted black-body radiation spectrum of just 0.1 percent, a hundred times better than the experiments carried out from rockets and balloons.

The final experiment is the diffuse-infrared-background experiment, designed to search for the radiation from primordial galaxies —that is, the first generation of objects to form after decoupling. By taking measurements at longer wavelengths than *IRAS* did, it is better suited to this task. After the epoch of transparency, matter in the universe was free to accumulate under the influence of gravity into the galaxies and clusters of galaxies. But how did this happen? Was the structure in the universe that would eventually reveal itself in the formation of galaxies already there in the primordial fireball? Or did something happen subsequently that caused galaxies to start to form, some 200 million years after the Big Bang? The formation of galaxies is expected to have produced a tremendous outburst of radiation that has not yet been detected; this is the task of the diffuse-infrared-background experiment.

The history of cosmology might well be divided into "B.C." (before *COBE*) and "A.C." (after *COBE*). After *COBE* we should know how the universe evolved after matter and radiation were decoupled in the early universe; we should know whether the universe is expanding uniformly, whether it is rotating, whether it is homogeneous or turbulent. We should know when and how galaxies were formed, and how and why they clustered. And if we understand all that, then we should be able to predict with some certainty the future evolution of the universe.

Infrared astronomy from space is probing the farthest citadels of the realm of Hephaestus. The gods cannot keep their secrets for long from the grasp of modern technology!

Interlude 3 • Space Works!

For those who have grown up in the Space Age, there is nothing novel in turning on one's television set in Europe to watch, live, the Super Bowl, or in tuning in from the United States to the Live Aid concert from the Wembley Stadium, London. We telephone friends and relations in the remote corners of the globe and are no longer impressed that they sound as if they are speaking from the next room. The improvements in forecasting weather that have been made possible from space are accepted with nonchalance, and no one is going to get too excited any longer by the beautiful images from space used to monitor the earth's resources—to check on ice cover, the effects of deforestation, river and ocean pollution, telltale indicators of the likely presence of minerals, the state of crops, etc. Perhaps we sleep more easily in our beds knowing that national security is improved by "spies in the sky," or knowing that the safety of loved ones in the air or at sea is enhanced by space navigation systems that pinpoint the position of ships and aircraft with great precision and can alert rescue services if distress signals are received. World commerce has been revolutionized by space communications; now the moguls of Wall Street and the City of London and the gnomes of Zurich can shift billions of dollars, pounds, francs, or ecus around the world at the touch of a key on a computer terminal. All these things may now be accepted as the norm. But, because of space, it is a very different world than a mere quarter-century ago. The space age has created a new "global village," putting all peoples in closer contact.

This book is about space *astronomy*; not space *applications*. Nevertheless, space science (in its various guises) and space applications cannot be separated entirely. The pioneering of space was achieved in large part for adventure, scientific, and political ends. Exploitation came later. Science is at the risk end of the business; commercial applications have largely followed the route marked out by scientific ventures. Thus, space could never have been used for commercial projects had not the early scientific missions first probed the nature of the near-Earth space environment. Fundamental research on the hazards of space (the radiation belts, the effects of solar radiation, the performance of machines operating in a near-zero-gravity environment, the impact of temperature extremes, etc.) was needed before any investor would have wanted to risk capital in a commercial space mission. New space technologies are continually demanded and developed by the space scientists, then used by commercial projects. Of course, one cannot claim that space applications would not have happened without space science, but they would have happened more slowly and less ambitiously.

Sometimes space pundits or politicians have tried to justify the enormous investment in space research on the basis of spinoffs— that is, the new technologies developed for space science that have been put to work in everyday life. Favorite illustrations are microcomputers and Teflon frying pans! Such arguments are rather flimsy, since the wide range of new technologies that have been spinoffs from space could have been developed far more cheaply without the space program, had their need been recognized. However, the spinoff from the space-science and space-adventure missions that might never have happened are the space-exploitation projects—the weather satellites, the communications satellites, the earth-resources satellites, the navigation satellites. It is a pity that the 30 percent of U.S. taxpayers who, even today, would wish to see investment in space research severely curtailed don't remind themselves of this fact. If the pioneering spirit to explore space for its own sake has been lost by some, then let us proceed in the knowledge that the history of space exploration shows that commercial exploitation inevitably follows along the path cleared by space science. It has been estimated that the investment in space science has found a hundredfold return in the commercial exploitation of space. For any venture, that represents an outstanding return on investment. Not that we should need to justify space science on these grounds, but it is surely a factor that needs to be remembered.

The first demonstration of transglobal television happened by accident. On the night of July 10, 1962, television relay stations at

Goonhilly Downs, Cornwall, England, and Pleumeur-Bordou, Brittany, France, picked up black-and-white images of the Stars and Stripes flapping in the breeze to the accompaniment of *The Star Spangled Banner*. The intent had been to demonstrate that TV signals could be bounced off *Telstar 1* between Maine and New Jersey, but the signals were unintentionally bounced across the Atlantic.

Telstar 1 was not only the first satellite dedicated to communications, it was also the first-ever commercial satellite (being financed by American Telephone & Telegraph). The first tentative experiments with communications via satellite burgeoned into a major business venture. With U.S. encouragement, the International Telecommunications Satellite Organization (Intelsat) was founded to establish a global communications network. Intelsat now has over 100 member states, although sadly the Soviet Union never joined (it has its own system, called Statsionar). Intelsat's first satellite was *Early Bird*, launched in April 1965. It was able to handle 240 telephone circuits or one TV service between the United States and Europe. The present generation of Intelsat satellites now spans the globe, and each handles tens of thousands of telephone calls and simultaneously several TV services. The real cost of transglobal communications continues to decline.

Another international organization in the communications business is the International Maritime Satellite Organization (Inmarsat), providing communications between ships at sea and between ships and land. Satellites are also exploited in a lifesaving role. Cospas/Sarsat is an international search-and-rescue service that uses equipment mounted on satellites for locating emergency transmitter beacons carried by aircraft, ships, and other vehicles. Since its inception, Cospas has helped to quickly locate crashed aircraft and disabled ships and has saved countless lives as a result. Its efficiency was demonstrated recently to a rather embarrassed Scottish yachtsman. He had removed his beacon from his boat and stored it on top of his wardrobe in his home, inadvertently activating it in the process. The signal was received by an orbiting Soviet satellite, and within a very short time police were knocking at the yachtman's door to satisfy themselves that he was not in distress.

All matter, whether living or nonliving, absorbs, reflects, and emits electromagnetic radiation. All substances possess a characteristic reflection or emission signature by which they can be

Space works!

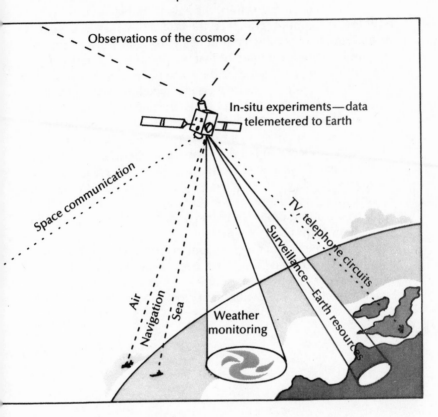

Observations of the cosmos

In-situ experiments—data telemetered to Earth

Space communication

TV, telephone circuits

Surveillance—Earth resources

Air

Navigation

Sea

Weather monitoring

identified. Earth-resources satellites gather this type of information
and relay it to ground stations for detailed analysis. There is a wide
range of applications for such data—for example, producing highly
accurate maps of even the most remote regions of the planet;
estimating the potential yield of crops and detecting crop disease;
monitoring the ecological balance; detecting oil slicks at sea, and
river and coastal pollution; and detecting likely areas to explore for
oil, minerals, and natural gas. One of the difficulties with the
earth-resources satellites is the issue of where monitoring ends and
spying begins. There is a certain understandable degree of
intergovernment suspicion of such activities, and no international
agency akin to Intelsat exists.

Pictures of cloud cover displayed nightly on TV weather forecasts are the best-known results from the advanced meteorological satellites now in orbit. However, the task of these satellites goes far beyond simply obtaining pictures of approaching snow storms or hurricanes (however important that might be). A vast range of other sensors are used to probe the atmosphere and to monitor the global climate system. Atmospheric temperature, water-vapor content, wind direction, atmospheric pressure, ocean currents, sea surface temperatures—all these important components of the weather system are measured from space. Some satellites are equipped to collect weather data from instruments on buoys and balloons. The advantage of monitoring the weather from space is that important data can be obtained from the remotest desert area or arctic wasteland. How many countless lives, or billions of dollars of rescued crops or protected property, have been saved by having a "weather eye" in space?

There are many other applications of space, and more are sure to follow. Remarkable things have been achieved, but in the exploitation of the space environment we are still mere novices. Space exploitation will continue to grow—because space works!

—— 4 ——
THE VISION OF APHRODITE

Ultraviolet radiation is familiar to us all, even though it lies outside our range of vision: It is the ultraviolet from the sun that is responsible for a suntan. Most solar ultraviolet radiation is in fact filtered out by the atmosphere, which is really rather fortunate, since exposure to too much ultraviolet can be harmful to life. Near-ultraviolet solar light (200–300 nanometers) is filtered out by the ozone layer. Without the ozone layer the level of solar ultraviolet radiation would reach dangerous levels; hence the concern that atmospheric pollution might destroy the ozone layer. Shorter-wavelength ultraviolet radiation is absorbed higher in the atmosphere. But from above the atmosphere, the vista revealed in ultraviolet light is one of majestic beauty—a vision of Aphrodite.

Just a year after Herschel had detected infrared radiation from the sun, the German Johann Ritter demonstrated the existence of solar ultraviolet radiation by producing a spectrum with a prism and noting the darkening of paper soaked in silver chloride and held in the invisible region of spectrum beyond the violet. Ultraviolet radiation with wavelengths from 300 to 400 nanometers does penetrate the atmosphere, so astronomers had been able to obtain a partial glimpse of the ultraviolet sky even before the advent of the Space Age. But access to the full ultraviolet horizon had to await the V-2s.

In 1946, Naval Research Laboratory scientists were given their first opportunity by United States Army colleagues to fly instruments on captured V-2s. Their first launch, from White Sands on June 28, 1946, carried an ultraviolet spectrograph. Photographic film, which was supposed to be recovered after the flight, was to be used to record ultraviolet spectra throughout the trajectory, thus measuring the atmospheric absorption of solar ultraviolet radiation at different altitudes. But things rarely went smoothly for the rocket pioneers. The launch was flawless, and the rocket soared to over 100 kilometers altitude; then it plunged earthward in accelerating streamlined flight, burying itself in an enormous crater in the New Mexico desert. Weeks of excavation produced a pile of twisted metal—but no film. The first ultraviolet astronomy record from space remains "archived" in its sandy grave. To avoid a repeat of this calamity, a reflight was planned for October 10, 1946, with the spectrograph mounted on the rocket's tailfin rather than in the nosecone. The idea was that the tailfin would be severed before reentry and that, with no aerodynamic properties, it would tumble gently to earth. And so it proved. This experiment of NRL's Richard Tousey recorded the first recoverable solar ultraviolet spectra from above the atmosphere, up to an altitude of 88 kilometers.

Astronomer Jesse Greenstein was one of the first to try to launch a high-resolution spectrograph to photograph the solar ultraviolet spectrum, in 1947. He wrote later, "I carried the instrument on the train to Johns Hopkins for tests and to White Sands [for the launch]; later I developed the recovered film back at Yerkes Observatory. The 10-inch-long strip was in excellent condition—it was completely unexposed! Thus I was probably the first classically trained astronomer to have an experiment fly, *and fail*, in space." Despite many such early setbacks, ultraviolet astronomy using rockets eventually started to pay dividends, and from rocket data NRL scientists were able to make a crude survey of the ultraviolet sky. Some ultraviolet astronomy was also undertaken from high altitude balloons.

As with other space-astronomy disciplines, the big break for ultraviolet astronomy came with the advent of satellites. A few hours of satellite observation matched that obtained from a decade of 50 rocket flights. First there were NASA's Orbiting Solar Observatory (OSO) satellites, the first of which was launched in 1962, with seven successors up until 1975. This highly successful series of spacecraft enabled detailed ultraviolet and X-ray studies of the sun. The Orbiting Astronomical Observatory (OAO) series of satellites was expected to prove just as successful for cosmic space astronomy. But the series was to prove ill-fated. OAO-1, launched in April 1966, suffered a catastrophic power failure on just its second day in orbit, before its telescopes could be directed heavenward. OAO-2 carried two ultraviolet experiments among its complement of seven instruments; they did work, and made useful progress. The third OAO failed at launch and had to be destroyed. The "good times" finally arrived for the OAO series in 1972, with the launch of a second version of the OAO-3 satellite; it was christened *Copernicus*, since 1972 was the 500th anniversary of the birth of the great Polish astronomer. Its contributions to ultraviolet astronomy were monumental. Also in 1972, the European Space Research Organization (later ESA) launched a very successful all-sky ultraviolet survey mission, code named *TD-1*; over 30,000 objects were cataloged in this first full survey of the ultraviolet sky.

As the *Einstein* mission meant that X-ray astronomy had truly come of age, ultraviolet astronomy can be said to have come of age with the *International Ultraviolet Explorer* (IUE) mission. IUE had its origins in the vision of U.K. space astronomer Bob Wilson. There was no prospect of the United Kingdom alone being able to fund a mission of the planned complexity (and cost) of what was originally called the *Ultraviolet Astronomical Satellite* (UVAS). So Wilson took his proposal to ESA. They rejected it. Undaunted by this (and other) setbacks, Wilson submitted his proposal privately to NASA via the Space Science Board of the United States National Academy of Sciences. The academy conducted a full assessment of the proposed mission, and they liked what they saw. NASA's Goddard Space Flight Center invited Wilson and his U.K. team to join them in a combined venture, which went through a metamorphosis to become the IUE. The United Kingdom was able to make a one-sixth contribution to the project. Eventually ESA also joined the project, at a similar level; it was a wise, if somewhat belated, decision, since IUE has proved to be arguably the most successful space-astronomy mission ever undertaken.

In the transition from UVAS to IUE, one very important change was agreed upon. It was decided to put the spacecraft in a geosynchronous orbit. In a geostationary orbit a spacecraft is in a circular orbit above the equator, with an orbital period of 24 hours. In a geosynchronous orbit, an elliptical orbit inclined at some angle to the equatorial plane is chosen, again with a 24-hour orbital period. For IUE the orbit is inclined 29 degrees to the equator. The 24-hour period means that it appears to hover over a region of the Atlantic Ocean and South America. IUE appears to trace out an irregular oval over the ground, but is always in sight of antennae linked to either the NASA control center at the Goddard Space Flight Center, or a European control center at Villafranca, near Madrid, Spain. For 8 hours a day, when the spacecraft is farthest to the northeast, ESA controls the spacecraft; NASA has control for

IUE orbital track. The oval approximates the ground track over which *IUE* flies during each orbit. Tick marks give 1-hour intervals.

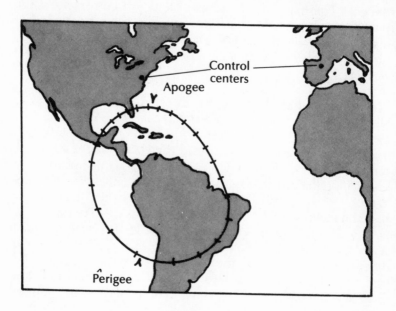

the remaining 16 hours. This orbit means that *IUE* can be operated much like an earthbound observatory. Astronomers can enjoy the tremendous flexibility in the control room previously enjoyed only by optical and radio astronomers—they can guide and update their observation programs directly at the console, while observations are being made. Unlike all previous major space missions, where experiments were run primarily for predesignated research groups (usually those who had built the instruments or provided data support), *IUE* has been operated from the outset as a "visiting observatory" for guest astronomers from the United States, the United Kingdom, and Europe. Here, in part, lay the secret of its success, and it is a great pity that so few of its successors have been planned to operate in this mode. All too often, it seems, space planners and instrument PIs fight jealously to preserve their own interests, not realizing that even in open competition they are likely to be amply rewarded for their endeavors. The "founding fathers" of *IUE* have all received the scientific kudos that are justly theirs, while opening up the facility freely to all astronomers able to get their observation proposals accepted by an allocation committee of peers.

NASA has played the major role in *IUE*. They were responsible for the spacecraft, the telescope and its spectrographs, the launch, and the operation of one of the control centers. As their contribution, the United Kingdom built the four televisionlike detectors used to record the spectra. ESA supplied the spacecraft's solar arrays and operates the second control room. Reflecting the major NASA role, U.S. astronomers are allocated two 8-hour observation shifts each day, and their colleagues across the Atlantic use the third shift each day.

The *IUE* carries a 45-centimeter aperture telescope, which can feed one of two spectrographs. One spectrograph operates in the long-wavelength region from 190 to 320 nanometers, and the other operates in the short-wavelength region from 115 to 200 nanometers. Each spectrograph can be operated in high resolution (that is, revealing greater spectral detail) or in low resolution (that is, with less spectral detail but able to detect fainter objects). Televisionlike vidicon cameras record the spectra to be transmitted to Earth. Star trackers on the spacecraft sample a field of 16 arc minutes in diameter, so that it is possible to determine precisely where the telescope is pointing.

The *IUE* spacecraft

IUE has operated almost flawlessly since its launch in January 1978. (Its original design life was three years—and even that period of operation is usually hailed as a success for a complex spacecraft.) In the intervening period it has had an 80-percent duty cycle (that is, 80 percent of its time has been spent doing astronomy)—an unprecedented record. The balance of the time is accounted for by engineering checks, maneuvering about the sky, and minor problems. The time actually gathering data can be compared with a ground-based telescope, at a good site, where with limited hours of darkness, uncertain weather, engineering requirements, etc., a 25 percent duty cycle, at best, might be possible. An important feature of *IUE* has been the interactive computer system at the control centers. This permits astronomers to complete a preliminary analysis of their data immediately after transmission to Earth at the end of an exposure. Thus quick decisions concerning later exposures can be made on the basis of an earlier exposure. Visiting astronomers are assisted in the control room by a spacecraft controller and a resident astronomer, both of whom are qualified to give expert advice and to sort out any problems. Redirecting *IUE* to different target objects is not a straightforward task. The spacecraft must be moved along a series of doglegs (making sure the sun, the moon, and the illuminated disc of the earth are avoided), instead of along the shortest path. The control room's computer helps plan necessary maneuvers, and observing schedules are planned to minimize the movements around the sky.

IUE has added a new dimension to the study of astronomy, and many astronomers would find it difficult to imagine life without it. Its observations have made a major impact on all areas of astronomical understanding, from planets, stars, and nebulae to galaxies and quasars.

It would be impossible to do justice to the scientific highlights of *IUE* in just a few pages; several volumes would be required. A selective summary must suffice.

IUE observed, in most cases for the first time, the ultraviolet spectra of nearly all the principal bodies in the solar system—the planets and many of their satellites, comets (including the recent apparition of Halley's comet), and asteroids. The ultraviolet data for asteroids led to a better understanding of the mineral assemblies present on asteroids.

The *Copernicus* mission made very important contributions to our understanding of the interstellar medium; its high-resolution spectroscopic capability was particularly well suited to such studies. *IUE* has complemented and extended the *Copernicus* research admirably. Studies of the interstellar medium are usually carried out using absorption-line spectroscopy. A bright continuum background source (say a luminous star) is observed; absorption features in its spectrum are produced by intervening interstellar material along the line of sight. The composition, density, and temperature of the interstellar medium, in various directions, have been probed using this technique. Highly ionized gas in the plane of the Milky Way has been studied. Knots of gas traveling at high velocity testify to the key role of violent phenomena such as supernova explosions in influencing the nature of the interstellar medium, and the remnants of ancient supernova explosions have been studied in considerable detail.

One of the most startling discoveries from *IUE* has been the detection of a hot gaseous halo surrounding the Milky Way, a galactic corona. The likely source of this hot gas is supernovae occurring near the central plane of the Milky Way. The hot gas in the halo, which extends out to distances of tens of thousands of light-years, appears to be rather clumpy. A favored analogy is a galactic fountain, squirting hot gas from supernovae out of the central regions of the galaxy, which cools and forms into clumps, then falls back toward the plane of the galaxy. It remains somewhat problematic how much of the universe's missing mass could be tied up in galactic coronae.

Using quasars or supernovae as background objects, astronomers have studied the interstellar medium in external galaxies. An intriguing detection has been a "bridge" of gas (first discovered in the radio spectrum) flowing between the Magellanic Clouds (the nearest galaxies) and the Milky Way. Bright stars in the Magellanic Clouds have been used to study their interstellar material and the gas in the outer halo of the Milky Way.

The contribution of *IUE* to the studies of stars has been especially important. Hot young stars emit most of their radiation in the ultraviolet and are thus well suited to study by *IUE*. But stars investigated have ranged from those in early stages of evolution right through to red supergiants. Important new information on mass-loss phenomena in stars has been found—that is, the mechanisms by which matter processed in the stars is fed back to the interstellar medium, via stellar winds, flaring or outburst phenomena, and explosions. The mass loss from bright young stars seems to be very irregular; rather than a steady "wind" of gas, shells of material appear to be ejected sporadically. The cause of such irregular behavior remains uncertain.

The so-called Wolf-Rayet stars are believed to have extreme mass, probably greater than 20 times the mass of our sun. These bloated giants are particularly unstable. *IUE* provided the first ultraviolet spectral data of a large sample of Wolf-Rayet stars, emphasizing their bizarre behavior. Some Wolf-Rayet stars appear to be in binary systems—but not all. Some are surrounded by ejected nebulae—but not all. Their common feature appears to be their high rate of mass loss.

Ground-based optical and infrared observations simultaneous with *IUE* observations resulted in the most detailed study ever conducted of novae explosions, verifying that they are probably produced by thermonuclear runaway explosions on the surface of a white dwarf. Simultaneous observations at radio, optical, X-ray, and ultraviolet wavelengths have also been obtained of several extragalactic supernovae, again leading to an improved understanding.

Ultraviolet observations of X-ray binaries, often made simultaneously with X-ray observations, have clarified the mass-exchange process whereby matter is transferred from the bright primary star to a compact companion, via an accretion disc. The ultraviolet light comes from the various components of the system—the primary star and its stellar wind, the gas flow and the accretion disc. By studying the varying X-ray, optical, and ultraviolet light throughout the binary system's orbit, these different components can be identified.

The ultraviolet spectra of normal galaxies are important in establishing their content of hot young stars (which emit primarily in the ultraviolet) and the rate at which new stars are being formed. Complementary optical, infrared, and ultraviolet data can be used to infer in some detail the stellar population of galaxies; again the *IUE* observations have been important in determining how the star content of galaxies evolves.

The strongest emission line in the ultraviolet is at a rest wavelength of 121.5 nanometers. This is the so-called Lyman-alpha emission line of hydrogen. When an ionized hydrogen atom (that is, a proton) combines with an electron, the electron falls rapidly to the lowest possible energy level in the atom, emitting a photon in the process. It is these photons that make up the Lyman series of emission lines, extending from 121.5 nanometers down to a wave-length of 91.2 nanometers. The Lyman-alpha line shows up very prominently in all sorts of astronomical systems, including active galaxies and quasars. Another strong emission line originates in carbon atoms that have lost three electrons, at a wavelength of 155 nanometers. Of course, in distant galaxies and in quasars the emission lines may show very significant red shifts. *IUE* has produced some intriguing insights into the nature of the active galaxies. One particular object, a bright Seyfert galaxy called NGC 4151, is the

Absorption features in the spectra of quasars may be due to (a) material ejected from the quasar, or, more probably, (b) material in faint galaxies lying along the line of sight.

(a)   (b)

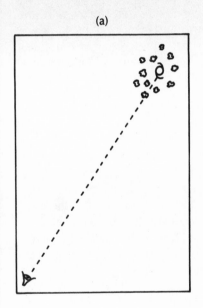
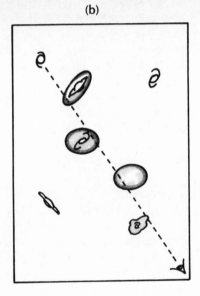

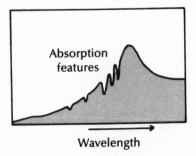

single object most often observed by *IUE*. There are several highly variable components in the ultraviolet emission that can be identified with various emitting regions in and around the Seyfert's core. Narrow absorption lines in the ultraviolet spectra of distant quasars are thought to be due to interstellar material in faint galaxies lying along the line of sight, as well as in the halo of the Milky Way.

By any measure, the *International Ultraviolet Explorer* represents an amazing success story. Few would have predicted its exceptional longevity, its "user-friendly" operation never before achieved in a space mission, or its fundamental contributions to almost all branches of astronomy. By these and other criteria, nothing has matched its success during the first three decades of the satellite age.

At wavelengths shorter than 90 nanometers, we enter the region commonly referred to as the extreme ultraviolet, or EUV. It was long thought that the EUV held little prospect for astronomical observation. Photons of wavelengths less than 91.2 nanometers have enough energy to knock the electron off a hydrogen atom (that is, to ionize it). In the process, the photon is absorbed. Since interstellar space is filled with atomic hydrogen (far and away the most common atomic species in the cosmos), EUV radiation from even the nearest stars is heavily absorbed. Only when one gets toward X-ray wavelengths does the transparency of interstellar space start to improve again. It seemed to many astronomers that there wasn't much point probing the universe in EUV radiation. But Stuart Bowyer from the University of California at Berkeley felt differently. (Remember, Bowyer worked with X-ray astronomy pioneer Herbert Friedman.) Despite the pessimistic view of his contemporaries, Bowyer managed to get a small EUV telescope on the joint U.S.-U.S.S.R. Apollo-Soyuz space mission, and found EUV emission from several nearby stars. Rocket payloads have confirmed these discoveries and made others. It seems that by sheer good fortune the sun lies in a region of the Milky Way where the density of the interstellar hydrogen is uncharacteristically low. It seems there might also be "holes" in the interstellar medium through which more distant EUV stars can be seen. The extreme ultraviolet cosmic landscape may not be as barren as astronomers had previously thought.

There are two missions that will explore the extreme ultraviolet toward the end of this decade. The first is an EUV telescope built by U.K. researchers to fly aboard the German-led *ROSAT* X-ray mission. The second is a NASA spacecraft instrumented by Bowyer's team from Berkeley called the *Extreme Ultraviolet Explorer*, *EUVE*.

EUV telescopes are, like X-ray telescopes, of grazing-incidence design. There are four telescopes on the *EUVE* spacecraft. Three of the telescopes are mounted to look radially outward from the spinning spacecraft so that they scan a circle in the sky for each revolution of the spacecraft. The spin axis of the spacecraft will always be kept pointing toward the sun, so that in six months the radially scanning telescopes will have surveyed the whole sky at EUV wavelengths.

The fourth telescope looks along the spin axis, away from the sun. This telescope will thus look at only a thin strip of the sky, but with extreme sensitivity. This fourth telescope is equipped also to measure spectra, and on completion of the all-sky survey, the spacecraft will be pointed at the brightest sources discovered so as to measure their spectra.

At present, fewer than 10 cosmic EUV sources have been discovered. This reflects the short survey time that has been possible from the Apollo-Soyuz mission and rocket flights. (Recall that prior to *Uhuru* only 30 X-ray sources had been discovered from a decade of rocket experiments, but now thousands of X-ray sources are known.) *ROSAT* and *EUVE* will certainly discover hundreds, if not thousands, of cosmic objects strong in extreme ultraviolet radiation. Known EUV sources include binary stars and hot white dwarfs. Other likely sources include supernova remnants, flare stars, novae, and the coronae of stars like the sun. If survey missions at other wavelengths are anything to go by, additional unexpected sources of EUV emission are sure to be found by *ROSAT* and *EUVE*. The EUV is one of the few remaining unexplored radiation regions, so the potential for discovery is high.

Perhaps the richest part of the electromagnetic spectrum lies in the region from 90 to 120 nanometers, the far ultraviolet. Every astrophysically important element has many emission lines in this range, and certain important species such as deuterium can be studied only here. The extreme richness of the spectrum allows detailed studies of the physical and chemical properties of various cosmic objects. A detailed understanding of solar-system objects, the interstellar medium, stars, nebulae, and galaxies and studies of crucial cosmological significance all demand access to the far ultraviolet. Yet only the *Copernicus* mission has explored this region, and then only with low sensitivity. So if the far ultraviolet is so important, why has it been so poorly studied? The reason is technical, since neither optical materials, which are transparent, nor coatings, which are highly reflective, are available over this wavelength range. It is for this reason that *IUE* stops just below 120 nanometers.

Reflecting telescopes usually use aluminum as the reflective coating. But pure aluminum rapidly oxidizes. While this doesn't seriously degrade the reflectivity of the telescope at optical wavelengths, the effect on ultraviolet wavelengths becomes serious. For this reason the reflecting elements in ultraviolet instruments are coated with a protective layer (magnesium fluoride in the case of *IUE*) that stops the aluminum from oxidizing. This cures one problem but produces another, since these protective layers result in seriously degraded effectiveness of the optics below about 115 nanometers. There seemed to be no simple technical solution to the problem. Nevertheless, the enormous importance of the far-ultraviolet region was widely recognized. NASA considered a mission called the *Far-Ultraviolet Spectroscopy Explorer* (*FUSE*), which was to use grazing-incidence optics to solve the reflectivity problem, but this required a very large (and expensive) spacecraft. ESA studied a mission called *Magellan*, which was to use a very basic optical system involving just a single reflective element, but this had rather limited performance. The United Kingdom considered a mission called the *Ultraviolet Space Observatory* (*UVSO*), which introduced the novel technology of coating the optics with pure aluminum in orbit, where if the spacecraft environment could be made clean enough the aluminum would not oxidize.

These various agencies soon realized that it made very little sense for them to be studying missions with the same scientific goals but with different technical solutions. In April 1983, a meeting was held in Windsor, England, where after some straight talking among officials of the space agencies it was agreed that the scientists from the United States and Europe should put their heads together to try to solve the scientific and technical challenges of far-ultraviolet astronomy. Shortly afterward a workshop was held in Annapolis, Maryland, where lengthy debate in the conference room and seafood restaurants led to agreement on the scientific objectives and technical options for a combined mission.

The new mission will be called *Lyman*. It is likely to be

launched in the mid-1990s, although there are various technical problems to be solved before construction can start.

One of the principal objectives of *Lyman* lies in the realm of cosmology and is of fundamental importance. It is to determine the cosmic abundance of deuterium (that is, heavy hydrogen). Deuterium is identical to hydrogen but contains a neutron in addition to the single proton. The origin of deuterium in the cosmos is believed to be the Big Bang, in which hydrogen, helium, and a small amount of deuterium were formed. Although deuterium is made in stars, it is easily destroyed again at the temperature experienced there, so stellar nuclear processes could not account for the presence of deuterium in the interstellar medium. It must have been created in the Big Bang, and the universe must then have cooled rapidly enough that the deuterium so formed wasn't destroyed. Its relative abundance will tell us something about the nature of the Big Bang and the rate of cooling of the expanding universe. Observing the abundance of the light elements is a powerful cosmological tool, since their relative quantities are linked to the conditions of the creation. The main design criterion for *Lyman* was accepted early in its planning: It must be sensitive enough and have sufficient spectral resolution to detect (in absorption from background quasars) the hydrogen and deuterium spectral lines in the halos of a reasonable sample of galaxies. If nothing else, astronomers are determined that *Lyman* will provide them with the capability to crack the deuterium problem and to measure its relative abundance with extreme precision. If we are ever to understand the nature of the Big Bang, we need to understand the abundance of deuterium.

IUE discovered significant populations of hot young stars in certain galaxies, including some ellipticals, where they were not expected. Access to the far ultraviolet will enable astronomers to better understand the nature of these young star populations. The point about elliptical galaxies is that they are thought to be relatively devoid of interstellar gas—just the substance from which young stars are born. So where can these young stars detected by *IUE* come from? Perhaps they are, in fact, old stars in binary systems rejuvenated by the transfer of matter from the companion star—an intriguing possibility that *Lyman* will investigate.

Quasars and the nuclei of active galaxies emit strongly in the far and extreme ultraviolet. Of course, the effect of red shift pushes these emissions toward longer wavelengths. But *Lyman* will have the task of understanding better the nature of the central power-house in these enigmatic objects.

The high spectral resolution and sensitivity of *Lyman* will be ideal for studies of the interstellar medium in the Milky Way and nearby galaxies such as the Magellanic Clouds and Andromeda. The *Copernicus* mission revolutionized our understanding of the local interstellar medium but was so limited in sensitivity that it could probe only the relatively bright nearby stars. *IUE* has made significant advances, but *Lyman* will be 100 times more sensitive than *IUE*. An important component of the interstellar medium, accessible to *Lyman* but not to *IUE*, is a tenuous hot component of the medium (at temperatures in excess of 100,000 degrees) in which cooler, denser clouds of gas are embedded. Molecular hydrogen (a hydrogen molecule is made up of two hydrogen atoms bonded together) will also be measured. As much as half the interstellar gas in the Milky Way might be in the form of molecular hydrogen.

The far ultraviolet is enormously important for studying stars, because of the wealth of emission lines in the far ultraviolet spectrum produced by the most abundant elements. *Copernicus* gave us a brief glimpse of a few stars in this wavelength region, but *Lyman* will be able to measure the far-ultraviolet spectra of stars some 14 magnitudes fainter. The study of stellar winds, planetary nebulae, supernova remnants, and interacting binaries will all be enhanced by access to the far ultraviolet.

For solar-system studies, the far and extreme ultraviolet have proved very important. Because the absorption problem at EUV wavelengths is insignificant within the confines of the solar system, EUV instruments have been flown on interplanetary missions such as *Voyager*. The atmospheres of the planets and their moons, and comets, all radiate diagnostically important emission lines in the far and extreme ultraviolet. Whereas the *Voyager* instruments could make just brief encounter studies of passing planets, the long lifetime planned for *Lyman*, and its extreme sensitivity, will allow for the first time detailed far- and extreme-ultraviolet studies in the solar system. The chemical evolution of the solar system is of special interest. In this regard Saturn's moon Titan warrants special attention: It is the only planetary satellite having a substantial atmosphere. Several hydrocarbons have already been detected and also nitrates, which could be prebiotic progenitors of biochemical compounds. Perhaps the chemistry of Titan might reveal the key to the evolution of complex biochemical compounds in the earth's atmosphere that were necessary for the evolution of life.

Ultraviolet astronomy from space will continue to flourish, since the physics and chemistry of any cosmic phenomena can be understood better in this radiation than in any other.

Interlude 4 • Athene and Truth

What is truth, and what is scientific fact? How certain are we that our present knowledge of the cosmos represents an ultimate understanding? Athene is the goddess of wisdom, but how wise are we about the forces of nature?

One can trace the path to an accepted scientific truth via the steps of faith, hypothesis, experiment, theory, and fact. There is always a large element of faith in science. Usually faith is thought of as part of religion, not science; however, in science we must accept a number of ideas on simple faith. They are ideas that we cannot test, we can in no way prove, but we must hold to be true. By faith the astronomer believes that the universe operates by one set of rules, which have acted uniformly throughout the cosmos since the creation. By faith it is accepted that these rules are not so mysterious that they cannot be understood through patient and persistent observation. Without this step of faith, the scientist would face an impossible task in unraveling the mysteries of the cosmos.

All science is concerned with making predictions based on patterns of behavior observed in the material world. For the astronomer, the patterns of behavior relate to cosmic objects and phenomena—stars, nebulae, and galaxies; pulsars, binaries, and quasars; and so on. A scientist pursues his observations using the so-called scientific method.

The scientific method begins with an observation of some feature or phenomenon in nature. A tentative idea, called a hypothesis, is suggested in an attempt to explain how the observation is to be interpreted. The only requirement of such a scientific hypothesis is that it can be tested; however fantastic a hypothesis might be, if it is testable then it is legitimate. In science if a hypothesis cannot be tested, it cannot be refuted and cannot be supported; it can only be ignored. Throughout the ages followers of all sorts of activities have called their subjects "scientific"; the sanction of science has been sought or simulated by various fringe disciplines, supposedly as a guarantee of authenticity. Astronomy has suffered more than most sciences in this regard, burdened with astrology, the occult, UFO mania, etc. It is essential that we are able to identify true scientific activities; the criterion of testability is a useful starting point.

The testing of a scientific hypothesis is by experiment. The experiment must be carefully thought out and designed so that the results of the experiment can be interpreted in a minimum of different ways. Of course, in astronomy, experiments (at least those beyond the solar system) must be carried out by remote observation, rather than by hands-on manipulation, probing, dissection, or destruction of the object under investigation. But the radiation emitted by celestial objects still enables their inner secrets to be revealed.

The results of an experiment are another set of observations. These new observations, added to the original ones, may form the basis of a new hypothesis to be tested by experiment. Thus, the more observations obtained, the better the chances of arriving at a satisfactory understanding of the original observations. Many circuits of the observation-hypothesis-experiment cycle might be required before such an understanding is reached. In astronomy this might involve different types of observation (for example, spectroscopy, polarimetry, and photometry) in different parts of the electromagnetic spectrum (say, X rays, radio waves, and visible light).

An understanding of how a group of observations might be interpreted and related to other observations is called a theory. A theory does not emerge automatically from the observation-hypothesis-experiment cycle, but requires insight and inspiration on the part of one or more scientists to produce a unifying concept. Sometimes a new theory is readily accepted by other scientists as soon as it is proposed, although more often it is subjected to vigorous discussion and further independent investigations. If a theory stands the test of experiments of many sorts and over a long period, it might eventually become established as a law stating an accepted scientific fact.

A problem in astronomy is knowing what to look for.

Astronomers often initially see only what they expect to see, rather than what is actually there. This is hardly surprising, since imagination is tempered by experience. How does one know what to look for, until you've found it? Certainly some things have been predicted, but most discoveries in astronomy have been made by accident during searches for unrelated phenomena. How could anyone have imagined a quasar, a pulsar, or an SS433 until they were discovered, essentially all by accident? Often it takes a new technology to reveal some unexpected phenomenon: Only when the unexpected has been revealed can the full scientific method be brought to bear to probe its true nature. Once a new type of object or phenomenon is discovered, then the world's telescopes will be turned on it to search, search, and re-search—to study its properties over the entire electromagnetic spectrum, using a variety of observational techniques, and to look for other examples, since nothing in the universe is thought to be truly unique.

But what of scientific truth? The ideas we hold, the scientific theories we accept, are not in themselves truths, but are human-made approximations of it. A scientific truth is not an absolute truth, but only a currently acceptable theory, originating from a faith that the universe operates by one set of rules that are within our ability to understand; the understanding develops from an initial observation which results in the repetitive cycle of hypothesis and experiment, and finally leads to a theory that is given respectability as a fact by acceptance over time.

There are a number of questions the cynic could ask about astronomical research and the pursuit of truth. For example, surely we are nearing the limit of all we can possibly know about the cosmos? This is what the great American astronomer Simon Newcomb asserted—in 1888! Just think what we have learned in the past century. The claim, by some, that we have gone about as far as we can expect to go is as absurd today as Newcomb's assertion was a century ago.

The cosmos is there forever, so shouldn't we slow down and wait for the more advanced technology of the future? This suggestion ignores the intimate connection between scientific curiosity and technological attainment. Better technology will not just evolve; we must lay down scientific challenges. If you stifle scientific curiosity, you turn off technological progress; it is as simple as that. This linkage has been graphically described by English philosopher Karl Popper: "The relationship between science and technology is like the progress of a man advancing through a swamp with his two legs labeled 'science' and 'technology.' First he painfully drags up one leg, puts it forward a little, and then puts it down; and then he does it with the other one. Neither leg is the leader or follower." It is no coincidence that the nations producing the most advanced technology are those that also invest heavily in curiosity-directed research.

Since the ultimate understanding of nature may be beyond the scope of human perception or understanding, why not give up now? That, surely, is a call for intellectual stagnation and would represent a one-way ticket back to the Dark Ages.

Okay, so astronomy represents an intellectual challenge. But shouldn't scientists be directing their curiosity and talents toward problems that need immediate solution or contribute to national security? Edward Teller, the Father of the Hydrogen Bomb, has spoken out often on a wide range of national policy issues. He has said, "There is no sharp line of division between applications in peace and war. Scientists may use the same tools to work on preventing war as they do to explore the great adventure of understanding how the universe began. Astronomy is also the part of science that has the oldest and most pervasive attraction to the nonspecialist. In the Space Age, it may be the natural gateway through which young people will enter into our wonderful and peculiar pursuits whose ultimate aim is understanding and simplicity, but whose short-range results may be to preserve peace and save freedom." We cannot be overly selective in the pursuit of knowledge. The various scientific and technical disciplines are closely linked, and a nation cannot hope to advance in certain areas of science and technology while ignoring others. You cannot sweep space research and astronomy aside and decide to concentrate on, say, the life sciences, or the technology of improved defense systems. The breakthroughs required in one scientific realm often come from a seemingly unrelated area. By supporting *all* science, one creates the intellectual environment within which *all* can flourish.

Aren't astronomers merely exploiting the extraordinary appeal to the public imagination of anything to do with space? There is no doubt that astronomy has a public recognition enjoyed by few other areas of science, and there seems to be a growing media appetite for astronomical information. Carl Sagan's "Cosmos" TV series approached the audience ratings of many soap operas, and glossy magazines featuring space and astronomy pack the newsstands. Obviously space astronomers have benefited enormously from this strong public interest in their trade, but it would be very unfair to claim that they have been unscrupulous in exploiting it. Nevertheless, those involved in astronomical research are a privileged elite; few could deny it.

In the era immediately after the Renaissance, astronomers were mainly gentlemen of private means or under the sponsorship of the nobility. They were motivated by a desire to gain an understanding of God's creation. Today, astronomers are more often than not ambitious young professionals, often motivated more by personal advancement than natural curiosity. So who are these modern-day Leonardo da Vincis? Well, most important, they are highly intelligent, highly qualified individuals. A doctorate from a top university is a minimum requirement for an aspiring astronomer or space researcher. That alone will represent six years or more of dedicated study. But even this is unlikely to qualify anyone for a permanent research post at a top scientific establishment in the highly competitive world of space astronomy. A research apprenticeship as a postdoctoral research assistant is often required. This gives an aspiring young researcher an opportunity to prove himself or herself, and to publish the results of original research (by which he or she will ultimately be judged) in the scientific journals. After that, there might just be the opportunity to get a permanent research post, but sadly that is far from guaranteed. Is it any wonder that those who survive this extended period of research training, indoctrination, and selection appear to be an elite? They have gone through a training required by few other professions and have had to acquire a wide range of scientific and technical skills. A young person entering college or university in his late teens would be lucky to be in permanent research employment before his thirties. The seekers of truth require real commitment. But for those who survive, the pursuit of the unknown represents an enormously rewarding endeavor. Research astronomers may be an elite, but they deserve to be.

Just what does the life of a professional astronomer and space researcher involve? To an outsider, it must appear to be a rather privileged existence. Salaries are usually relatively good (especially for someone doing something with high job satisfaction), and working hours are flexible. There is plenty of foreign travel and the opportunity to attend scientific conferences in exotic locations.

Egos are fed by broad media interest in those "pushing back the frontiers of knowledge," and public recognition and interest are high. All these assertions are true, in part, but a more balanced assessment is required. Salaries may be adequate, but they rarely recognize the long years of training (with minimal financial support) before a research scientist realizes an acceptable earning potential. Work hours may be flexible, but for a top researcher to stay at the top necessitates long hours of work. There may be plenty of travel (often too much!), but forefront research should, and usually does, involve the frequent exchange of results and ideas: Conference synergism is an essential component of scientific progress. While science does enjoy a high public profile, and egomania might sometimes appear to be the dominant driving force for certain individuals, the vast majority of researchers still retain the Renaissance spirit to explore the unknown.

In the end, Athene will have her way. Wisdom will prevail, since the pursuit of knowledge is an indelible part of the human spirit. Administrations come and go; funding policies swing from generosity to stinginess; technological advancement waxes and wanes; national priorities change. But throughout it all, the curiosity of humankind remains. Science *is* a noble cause. The attempt to understand the nature of the universe, and our celestial heritage, is a challenge comparable to the most courageous exploits of adventurers throughout the ages who sought to explore the unknown. It is the capacity of men and women to understand and utilize their terrestrial environment that has set them apart from other earthly creatures. Perhaps it will be their capacity to partially understand their universal environment as they seek their ultimate "roots" among the stars that may eventually set them apart from other celestial civilizations.

—— 5 ——
MIGHTY CYCLOPS

CARRYING OUT OPTICAL ASTRONOMY FROM THE GROUND CAN be a frustrating business, as any astronomer will tell you. Getting to use one of the world's major telescopes is a highly competitive task. Under the peer-review system of time allocation practiced at most observatories (in which a committee of astronomers sits in judgment on the proposals of their fellow researchers), even an observation program of outstanding merit might be assigned only a few nights of precious telescope time each year. If one could be guaranteed cloud-free skies, and perfect visibility, this might suffice. Unfortunately, all too often hard-won observation time is lost under cloudy skies; and even when weather conditions allow, distorted images arising from atmospheric turbulence may frustrate the scientific objectives. Ground-based astronomers will *always* suffer from poor weather (even at observatories in temperate latitudes), poor visibility caused by atmospheric conditions (even at the best mountaintop sites), and contaminating light, both natural —for example, lightning—and man-made—for example, city lights (even at the most remote observatories). No telescope can *ever* realize its full technical potential under the perturbing atmosphere, nor can it access the astrophysically important ultraviolet and infrared radiations adjacent to the visual band, because of atmospheric absorption. If only one's telescope were *above* the confounded atmosphere, in a perfectly dark sky free of turbulence and contamination!

Immediately after World War II, Princeton astronomer Lyman Spitzer advanced the idea of a large space telescope, a world-class facility of a size exceeding that of even the magnificent 100-inch telescope on Mount Wilson (then the world's largest telescope). Three decades would pass before the concept would receive congressional approval, and four decades before it could be placed in orbit from the space shuttle. These four decades have been a time of intense "astropolitical" lobbying, on-again, off-again decision making, major technical and management challenges and changes, and investment of more than a billion dollars! But few astronomers would regret the frustrations endured, or question the enormous effort and budget. (Whether the politicians have regrets is another matter!) If one were looking for the *ultimate* in telescopes, then the *Hubble Space Telescope* would come close to it—the "giant eye in the sky," mighty Cyclops.

The first official mention of what originally became known as the *Large Space Telescope* (*LST*) was in a 1962 report on the future of space science by the National Academy of Sciences (NAS). An *LST*, with a 120-inch aperture, was identified as a logical long-term goal for space astronomy. The recommendation was repeated in an NAS report three years later. But this time the academy decided to act on its recommendation, setting up a committee chaired by Spitzer to define the scientific objectives of *LST*. The space enthusiasts were convinced of the enormous potential of a large telescope above the atmosphere, but the response from many in the optical-astronomy community was muted. Exciting things were happening on the ground. Spectacular new discoveries were being made. New ground-based facilities were being planned. One could build tens of large ground-based telescopes for the cost of just one in space. (The eventual capital cost of the Hubble Space Telescope would exceed the combined total for the world's top 40 ground-based telescopes!) Few traditional ground-based astronomers were about to commit themselves strongly to a project likely to take at least 20 years to be realized and which might not even be in orbit during their research careers. But *LST*, and Spitzer, just wouldn't go away.

The next NAS review of the future needs and priorities for astronomy (from space *and* the ground), chaired by Jesse Greenstein of Cal Tech, was reported in 1972. *LST* was again identified as a realistic and desirable long-range goal for astronomy, but it was placed at a lower priority than a number of new ground-based facilities and an advanced space observatory for X-ray astronomy. Top priority was given by the Greenstein committee to a very large array of radio telescopes (the so-called VLA, subsequently built in New Mexico); second priority was a program for new electronic detectors and large ground-based optical telescopes; third priority was the development of infrared astronomy; and fourth priority was the X-ray astronomical observatory. *LST* was one of a group of projects rated at lower priority.

If traditional astronomy was only lukewarm about *LST*, at least top NASA management was showing some enthusiasm. In the aftermath of Apollo, they desperately needed large, prestigious projects. *LST* was just the type of challenge they wanted. In 1972 the space agency went as far as to designate its Marshall Space Flight Center, in Huntsville, Alabama, as the focal point for *LST* activities; the widely respected young director of the Yerkes Observatory, Bob O'Dell, was hired as the lead scientist for the project. In fact, NASA's support for *LST* was to wax and wane during the early years.

By 1973, NASA had selected a working group of scientists from several academic institutions to begin a preliminary design study of the telescope and its instruments. But the group was constrained to work within NASA's meager financial resources for advanced planning. Congress would need to approve the project and earmark funds for more detailed studies. Few had realized what a reluctant patron Congress would initially prove to be.

The early seventies was a bad time for NASA to be seeking funding for any major new project. After the initial excitement of the Apollo program, public interest in space had diminished. Opinion polls indicated that over half the population wanted to see substantially *less* money invested in space; less than 20 percent wanted to see an increased investment. Presidents Kennedy and Johnson had shown enthusiasm for science in general and for space in particular; but President Nixon's lower opinion of science was well known (symbolized by his abolition of the office of presidential science adviser). U.S. politics was reeling from the multiple body blows of Vietnam, campus and inner-city unrest, the first oil crisis, and Watergate. "Big Science" was hardly atop the popularity polls, and *LST* was *big* Big Science. And alas, the solid scientific lobby needed for a project of this scale was lacking. *LST* did figure in NASA's 1974 submissions to a congressional subcommittee on appropriations, but when the appropriations bill was sent to the full House of Representatives in June 1974, all funds for the *Large Space Telescope* had been deleted. The report stated, "The Committee notes that the *LST* is not among the top four priority telescope projects selected by the National Academy of Sciences, and suggests that a less expensive and less ambitious project be consid-

ered as a possible alternative." Recovery from this disastrous position would severely test the wit, wisdom, and patience of the
advocates for LST.

Leading the rear-guard action for a space telescope were the
ubiquitous Lyman Spitzer and a Princeton colleague, John Bahcall. The Princeton lobby displayed enormous energy and resolve,
and considerable political acumen, in winning first the hearts and
minds of their astronomical colleagues and eventually the hearts
and dollars of Congress. Their first task was to account for the
priority ordering in the Greenstein report, which placed LST
among lower-priority projects. Spitzer and Bahcall solicited new
support from all 23 members of the Greenstein committee and got
them to agree to a statement drafted by Bahcall: "In our view *Large
Space Telescope* is the leading priority among future new space-
astronomy instruments." The statement was sent to selected congressmen. Greenstein was moved to have his own interpretation of
his committee's report entered into the *Congressional Record*: "I am
confident that had we not had in mind budget limitations, at-the-
time-unsolved technological problems, and had we fully realized
the wide range of discovery that we had even in the last three years,
we would not have taken quite so 'conservative' an attitude. [The
LST] will open up new and imaginative vistas for the human mind
to contemplate." Such was the power of Spitzer's and Bahcall's
advocacy that even many from the most cautious sector of the U.S.
astronomical community were gradually won around to support
publicly (if not always privately) the LST project. Important allies
were won in Europe, where some astronomers expressed an interest in working toward a European participation in the mission.
Despite the many public proclamations for LST, however, there
remained divisions between the strong supporters of space astronomy and those, generally of an older generation, who continued to
place top priority on ground-based projects. The schism remains
even today throughout the global scientific community.

So much for the astronomical fraternity. Now for Congress.
During the late summer and in the fall of 1974, Spitzer and Bahcall visited and wrote to influential congressmen and encouraged
other astronomers to lobby NASA and the politicians. As a federal
civil servant, Bob O'Dell was unable to participate directly in the
Capitol Hill escapade, although there is little doubt that he was in
close contact with the Princeton campaigners. Political allies were,
at last, being attracted to the cause—most notably Senator Charles

Mathias of Maryland, who played a crucial role. Eventually the funding skirmish was won, and the Senate Appropriations Sub-committee agreed to restore $6.2 million for *LST* planning studies. But the battle was not yet over. On August 9, 1974, President Nixon resigned, and President Ford implemented an immediate government austerity program. The *LST* study budget was slashed by half, and the directive was issued "that consideration [be] given to substantial participation of other nations in a less expensive project to be launched at a later date." The new president and the Congress were now saying in effect, that there would be a space telescope, but it wouldn't be a *large* space telescope, it wouldn't be an exclusive U.S. venture, and it wouldn't be given accelerated funding. Spitzer's dream had been reduced in scope and delayed, but not destroyed.

In 1977, NASA appointed a new team of 60 leading scientists to participate, under O'Dell's direction, in the detailed design and development of a space telescope. The team included instrument builders, telescope designers, specialists in spacecraft operations and data handling, and several interdisciplinary scientists who would advise on the complementarity of the scientific objectives of the space telescope and those of other astronomical facilities on the ground and in space.

Congress formally approved the space telescope in 1978. (The *large* had now been dropped from the name, in a symbolic gesture to Congress's insistence that the project be cut back; later, in recognition of the monumental contributions to astronomy of Edwin Hubble, the project was named the *Edwin P. Hubble Space Telescope, HST.*) By the time of formal approval, preliminary designs of the telescope had been completed and the cost of the project estimated (although significant cost escalations would follow). The original 120-inch aperture was now a 94-inch aperture. The telescope of *HST* uses a 94-inch concave primary mirror, with a small convex secondary mirror 16 feet in front of the primary mirror and directing light back through a hole in its center to a focus where the various scientific instruments are placed.

The task of producing the most precise and accurate telescope ever constructed fell to the Perkin-Elmer Corporation of Danbury, Connecticut. An enormous amount of work (some 4 million person-hours) went into the ultra-accurate mirror manufacture. Opticians had to devise novel methods of pushing optical technology to new limits; indeed, the production of the space telescope's mirror is an excellent example of space science presenting technology with major new challenges from which spinoff technologies eventually evolve.

The primary mirror was made from ultra-low-expansion (ULE) glass; because of the temperature extremes endured in space, a material that suffered minimal distortion with changing temperature was required. The disc from which the mirror would eventually be formed was fabricated from square cells of ULE with honeycomb cores, fused together. Two 1-inch-thick sheets were fused to the front and back of the 12-inch-thick honeycomb structure separating and supporting them. Because of the honeycomb structure, this disc weighed just a quarter as much as a solid disc of glass of the same diameter. The space-telescope mirror weighs less than 1 ton, compared with the 14 tons of the primary mirror of the Mount Palomar 200-inch telescope. (The whole *HST* spacecraft weighs about 11 tons.)

The challenge was to shape the primary mirror (called *figuring* in opticians' parlance) to an accuracy of at least 1/80 of a wavelength of helium-neon laser light—an accuracy referred to as *1/80 wave*. Most large telescope mirrors are good to only about 1 wave. As if the specification itself weren't challenging enough, there was another major requirement. The *HST* will operate in a weightless space environment, but of course the mirror was to be figured and polished on the earth: The pull of terrestrial gravity would have created an unacceptable error. (If the mirror had been supported at its periphery, the center would have sagged by 17 waves—over a thousand times the required accuracy!) To overcome this problem, a zero-gravity simulator was designed. A support mechanism was built using 138 support rods, with each rod exerting a precisely known force on the back surface to offload a region of the mirror by exactly its own weight. It took 50 engineers three years to build the zero-gravity simulator. Only then could figuring and polishing of the primary mirror begin.

The figuring process used a computer-controlled polisher, working repeatedly over surface bumps and high points. After each polishing run, the surface was measured with a laser and a contour map was produced highlighting the imperfections. This contour map was then used to program the computer-controlled polisher to spend more time polishing the high points on the next run. Caution was the keynote, since glass once removed could not be put back on the mirror. During the 28 months of polishing, 200 pounds of material were removed from the mirror. The final precision must be emphasized; the deviation from the ideal contour was less than 10 nanometers. The accuracy of the final figuring of the primary is such that if the mirror were scaled to the size of the United States, no hill or valley would depart more than 2½ inches from the mean surface. The task of figuring the secondary mirror was equally demanding.

The next task was to coat the mirror with aluminum to give it its reflective surface. This is done quickly under high vacuum. But the aluminum quickly oxidizes when exposed to the atmosphere. This is not a major problem at optical wavelengths, but aluminum oxide seriously degrades the performance of the mirror at the ultraviolet wavelengths accessible from space. To stop the aluminum from oxidizing, a thin coating of magnesium fluoride was deposited over the aluminum. The thickness of the aluminum (0.01 microns) and magnesium fluoride (less than half this thickness) had to be extremely uniform. This was a very difficult assignment, but it was again carried out with remarkable precision. The accuracy of the mirrors gives the HST a resolution of 0.1 seconds of arc—equivalent to resolving the left and right headlights of a car in California viewed from New York.

The structure to support the mirrors was fabricated by Boeing Aircraft Company using graphite-fiber-reinforced epoxy, a strong, lightweight material highly stable over a wide temperature range. The positions of the mirrors (effecting the focus of the telescope) can be remotely adjusted with extreme precision.

The telescope assembly, once completed by Perkin-Elmer, was shipped to Lockheed Missiles and Space Corporation of Sunnyvale, California, who had the task of integrating the telescope with the spacecraft support systems, such as power supplies and computers. The *Hubble Space Telescope* was due to be launched in October 1986. The *Challenger* disaster destroyed that prospect. However, it was decided that HST would be the first scientific payload to be placed in orbit on recommencement of the shuttle program.

In observing power, the HST improves on large ground-based telescopes to the same extent, approximately, that Galileo's first telescope for astronomical observations improved on the capability of the unaided eye. Shortly after turning his telescope to the heavens for the first time in 1609, Galileo wrote, "I have seen stars in myriads which have never been seen before, and which surpass

Launched from the space shuttle, the *Hubble Space Telescope* will revolutionize space astronomy into the twenty-first century.

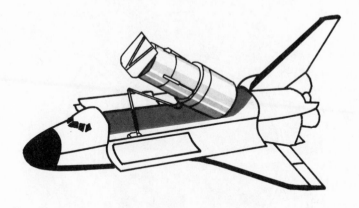

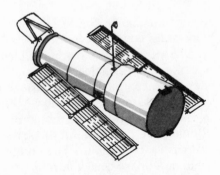

the old previously known stars in number more than ten times."
His astronomical descendants will now look at the universe with
comparable awe using a telescope the power of which Galileo
could not even have imagined. Just as Galileo made discoveries
not previously envisaged (mountains on the moon, satellites
around Jupiter, etc.), the most spectacular discoveries by the *Hubble Space Telescope* are likely to be objects and phenomena that
have not been predicted.

The focal plane of *HST,* showing the central pick-off mirror for the single radial instrument (the WFPC), the entrance apertures for the four axial instruments, and the three outer mirrors forming part of the fine guidance sensor system

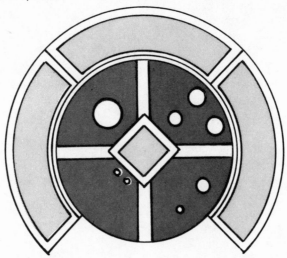

The development and capital cost of *HST* was a mind-boggling $1.2 billion. Operating costs will add a further $60 million per year, so that the telescope's original cost is doubled after 20 years in orbit. The program drew in a major way on the technology developed for the Key Hole spy satellites. What would the cost have been without this background technology? President Reagan's science adviser, George A. Keyworth, observed, "I have no idea how much it would have cost to build this telescope if there had never been a military space program. The number is, I suspect, so vast that we would never have been able to do it."

Five major scientific instruments are available on *HST* during its first few years of operation. However, the intention is that instruments will be changed every five years or so in orbit. *HST* is designed to remain in orbit for 15 years but will probably be operational for several decades. The space shuttle could bring it down to Earth for major refurbishment and upgrade, or perhaps such major servicing could be done in orbit on the planned space station. Although the telescope is designed for optimum performance in the ultraviolet, optical, and infrared wavelengths, the first-generation instruments are restricted to the ultraviolet and visible spectra. No doubt instruments specifically for infrared astronomy will be included in later payload changes.

Of the five instruments, four are mounted in axial quadrants at the focal plane of the telescope; the fifth is mounted radially, at the side of the telescope. The image of any object can be directed toward any one of the four axial instruments, or to a central mirror fixed at 45 degrees and directing light to the single radial instrument.

Let us start with the radially mounted instrument called the wide-field/planetary camera (WFPC). It is designed to take pictures of astronomical fields, with varying spatial resolution (that is, varying degree of detail; *spatial resolution* refers to the ability to distinguish closely spaced features). The WFPC can be used in two modes—one to image large fields with modest spatial resolution, and the other to image small fields (such as individual planets) at high resolution. The imaging device for each mode is a mosaic of four charge-coupled devices (CCDs), which are detectors ideally suited to the measurement of faint light levels. A CCD is a form of silicon chip that converts incident light photons into stored electrical signals. Each highly sensitive CCD chip on the WFPC is divided into 640,000 individual picture elements (pixels); that is, 800 pixels on a side. The mosaic of four CCDs therefore contains 2.5 million pixels. The electrical signal from each pixel is proportional to the number of photons acquired by that pixel during an exposure. In the wide-field mode each pixel is of side 0.1 arc second and the field of side 2.67 arc minutes; in the planetary mode each pixel is of side 0.043 arc seconds and the field of side 68.7 arc seconds (adequate to image all the planets, although the camera will also be used in this mode for imaging many extended objects, such as galaxies and nebulae). In the clarity of space one is free of the image distortion caused by atmospheric turbulence; resolution is limited merely by the telescope to less than 0.1 arc second.

The WFPC is sensitive to wavelengths from 115 nanometers, in the far ultraviolet, to 1,100 nanometers, in the near infrared. CCDs are naturally sensitive to visible and infrared photons; sensitivity in the ultraviolet has been achieved by coating the CCDs with an organic phosphor called coronene that converts ultraviolet photons to visible light, which CCDs can detect. Ultraviolet and near-infrared imaging, impossible from the ground, can thus be carried out.

One of the most exciting tasks for the WFPC is to search for

The WFPC. Light enters the instrument via the pick-off mirror; the incoming beam is split into four by a pyramidal mirror, and each beam is then fed to separate CCD cameras. There are eight CCDs in all, four for each mode of operation.

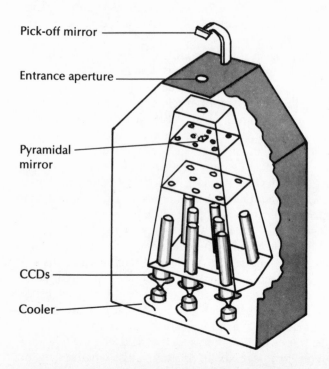

Pick-off mirror

Entrance aperture

Pyramidal mirror

CCDs

Cooler

planetary systems around nearby stars. Do planetary systems form naturally around all stars? If so, presumably the nature of some such planets must be Earthlike, on which life forms will have evolved. The WFPC cannot detect the planets themselves, but gravitational wobble of a star would indicate the presence of a companion or planetary system.

The WFPC will also study distant quasars, thought to be the superbright nuclei of certain young galaxies, to see whether the faint, diffuse light from the surrounding galaxies can be detected. Between these two extremes is a vast range of exciting projects— for example, imaging rich clusters of galaxies to find supernovae (many per week can be discovered, compared with the 10 or so

found per year from the ground). High-resolution imaging of galaxies will resolve stars, planetary nebulae, supernova remnants,
hydrogen nebulae, etc., the details of which it is impossible to
resolve using ground-based telescopes. An important question is
whether galaxies at remote distances (seen as they were when the
universe was only a fraction of its present age) are arranged in
clusters, as are those located much closer to us. One theory of
galaxy formation requires that they are born in clusters; another
suggests that clustering occurred later as the universe expanded.
WFPC observations should resolve this question.

The WFPC will be the busiest of the *HST* instruments, since,
even when the use of the telescope is dedicated to one of the other
instruments, the WFPC can be used in a serendipitous mode.

One of the axially mounted instruments has been supplied by
the European Space Agency. Following Congress's request that the
project be pursued on an international basis, negotiations between
NASA and ESA resulted in the Europeans taking a 15-percent
stake in the mission. ESA provided the solar panels for powering
the spacecraft, plus the scientific instrument. The ESA instrument
is called the faint-object camera (FOC). Its performance comple-
ments that of the WFPC, being capable of detecting extremely
faint objects; the FOC exploits the full optical power of the *HST*.
Two independent optical systems are used—one to form images of
exceptionally high resolutions (pixel side 0.022 arc seconds, field of
side 11 arc seconds), the other with more modest resolution (pixel
side 0.044 arc seconds, field of side 22 arc seconds) but still comparable to the best resolution of the WFPC. Each optical system has
as its detector an image-intensifying device similar to the light-sensitive tube in a television camera. The detector is designed to count
individual photons acquired in each pixel. It is particularly sensitive to ultraviolet and blue wavelengths. In addition to producing
images of very faint objects, the FOC also has a modest spectroscopic capability and can measure polarization.

The faint-object camera will be the obvious choice when observations with the highest possible spatial resolution are needed. For
example, when a dense cluster of stars is photographed from the
ground, it is impossible to resolve individual stars at the heart of
the cluster. The study of stars in a cluster is enormously important
in stellar evolution research, since in a cluster we have a large
sample of stars that are believed to have been born at the same time
and to have similar initial chemical composition, and that are all at

roughly the same distance (so there is no uncertainty about their relative intrinsic brightness). The stars in a cluster are of varying initial mass, from stars much smaller than the sun to stars very much more massive. The evolution of a star depends critically on its mass. Simply counting stars of different types (that is, of different masses) in a cluster will tell us a great deal about the accuracy of our models of stellar evolution. The high resolution of the FOC enables us to do this in even densely populated clusters.

Even above the densest part of the atmosphere, one has not escaped entirely sources of light contamination; the problems of the zodiacal light and scattered moonlight and starlight remain. Background light contamination thus competes with the light from the most distant (and therefore faintest) objects in the universe that one is trying to detect. Here is where the small pixel size of the FOC is so important, since the smaller the pixel the smaller the amount of contaminating light competing with the desired detection of a faint point source. Thus the FOC is able to detect objects very much fainter than could ever be detected from the ground, even with the largest telescope; indeed, objects at least 50 times fainter should be seen. The universe accessible to the *Space Telescope* has a volume 350 times larger than can be observed with the best ground-based telescope. Since when we look out into the cosmos we are also looking back in time, the *HST* can see further toward the Big Bang than any other optical telescope. The range of science performed by the FOC embraces everything from the nearest stars to the most distant quasars.

The first of the two spectrographs on *HST* is called the faint-object spectrograph (FOS). It is designed to perform spectroscopic observations, with modest resolution, of extremely faint objects at ultraviolet and visible wavelengths (115–800 nanometers). After the incoming light is spread out into a spectrum by a grating, it passes through an intensifier and is then detected by a linear array of 512 light-sensitive diodes. There are two such detectors—one sensitive to ultraviolet and blue light, the other working at the red end of the spectrum. In addition to measuring spectra of extremely faint objects (much fainter than one could ever hope to take spectral observations of from the ground), the FOS has two additional important features; for comparatively bright objects it is able to measure polarization, and it can detect extremely rapid spectral variations (on time scales as short as milliseconds).

Obtaining spectra of the faintest, most distant objects in the universe (quasars and galaxies in formation) is, of course, enormously important. However, plans for the FOS are not restricted merely to faint objects in the early universe. The optical pulsars in our own galaxy are very faint objects, as are certain interesting dwarf stars. The faintest filaments in supernova remnants and other nebulae will be investigated in a way not previously possible. Some of the most important astrophysical information is revealed in the ultraviolet portion of the electromagnetic spectrum, and ultraviolet spectroscopy from earlier space missions (*Copernicus* and the *International Ultraviolet Explorer*) revealed previously unknown phenomena that will now be studied in greater detail with *HST*—for example, the giant halo of hot gas surrounding the Milky Way discovered by *IUE*.

When higher spectral resolution is required, this is provided by the third axial instrument, the high-resolution spectrograph (HRS). There is a price to be paid for higher spectral resolution in a spectrograph: If the incoming light is spread out more widely in a spectrum, then there will be fewer detected photons per detected spectral element. Quite simply, higher resolution means lower sensitivity. The HRS provides spectral information only for objects 60 times brighter than can be recorded with the FOS.

The HRS has six interchangeable gratings to spread out the light into a spectrum. Each grating covers a fixed range of wavelengths in the ultraviolet, between 115 and 320 nanometers. It is a particularly powerful instrument for studying the interstellar gas in the Milky Way and other galaxies. These observations are often complicated by the random motions of different gas clouds; varying Doppler shifts result in various spectral features being blurred if one uses only modest spectral resolution. Detailed studies of stellar atmospheres are also possible, particularly in massive stars where the stellar winds (the flux of gas continually emitted at high velocity by certain stars) can be observed and in binary systems where a flow of gas between the stars is detected. In such studies the HRS will rule supreme.

The final axial instrument on *HST* is called the high-speed photometer (HSP). This is designed to provide highly accurate measurements of the intensity of light (over a range of 115 to 650 nanometers) from astronomical objects. Time variations as rapid as 10 *micro*seconds (that is, 10 millionths of a second) can be detected with HSP. Such short variations would be obliterated by the atmosphere if an attempt was made to detect them from the ground. (In fact, the detector for the HSP, called an image-dissector scanner, has been used extensively in ground-based astronomy but can only realize its full potential from space.) Although the HSP is the simplest instrument on the space telescope (it has no moving parts, using the pointing precision of the spacecraft to direct light into one of its 100 combinations of filters and entrance apertures), its range of exciting uses is enormous.

The ability to distinguish events separated by a mere 10 microseconds implies that variations of light output of a star as small as 3 kilometers across could be detected. Such rapid variations might be expected from material spiraling into a black hole, just before disappearing over the so-called event horizon beyond which light cannot escape from the black hole's gravitational field. Rapid pulsations from other compact systems (pulsars, X-ray binaries) will also provide interesting results about the detailed physical processes underlying their behavior.

The exceptional pointing precision of the HST is achieved using devices called fine guidance sensors. These lock onto the images of guide stars falling in an annulus outside the central portion of the focal plane of the telescope used by the scientific instruments. The extreme accuracy of the sensors is better than 0.01 seconds of arc. (Imagine holding a 300-kilometer fishing rod so steady that its remote end never moved by more than 1 centimeter; that is the equivalent pointing accuracy of HST!) In fact, at any one time only two of the three fine guidance sensors are needed to control the telescope; the third can be used to accurately measure stellar positions, for a research field called astrometry. In astrometry the positions of the stars are determined with maximum precision; these accurate positions can be used to estimate the distances to nearby stars (using a technique called trigonometric parallax) and to estimate their motions across the sky.

There is a computer on the spacecraft to control the operation of the observatory and handle the flow of data. Astronomers will communicate with the space telescope by means of the NASA Tracking and Data Relay Satellite System (TDRSS), a series of satellites in geostationary orbit that act as relay stations between spacecraft in low Earth orbit (like HST) and NASA ground stations. Thus even when HST is below the horizon from its control center at the

Goddard Space Flight Center, outside Washington, DC, communication will always be maintained via TDRSS. There are various observing constraints on the telescope: It must always be pointed at least 50 degrees away from the sun and 15 degrees away from the sunlit moon and Earth. Thus planning an efficient sequence of observations provides quite a headache for the schedulers.

The observation program for the space telescope is administered for NASA by the Association of Universities for Research in Astronomy (AURA). AURA is a consortium of 17 universities, organized originally to operate various U.S. national ground-based astronomical observatories. After data is received at the Goddard Space Flight Center (where some preliminary data reduction can be performed) it is transmitted to the Space Telescope Science Institute, which was set up by AURA at the Johns Hopkins University campus in Baltimore; data is also sent to a corresponding facility run by ESA in Munich, Germany.

The first director of the Space Telesope Science Institute (which has a staff of 240) is none other than Riccardo Giacconi, "patron saint" of *Uhuru, Einstein,* (and *AXAF*). Giacconi's appointment was greeted with some surprise by many of the old guard of astronomy, but was warmly welcomed by those who knew of his contagious enthusiasm and dynamic management style. The institute's mandate is very specific: "to provide the tools for the most efficient utilization of the *Edwin P. Hubble Space Telescope* by the astronomical community." If anyone could provide the tools and guarantee efficient utilization, it was Riccardo Giacconi.

To carry out its wide range of responsibilities, the Space Telescope Science Institute is divided into various branches. For example, there is the Instrument Support Branch, whose task is to monitor the performance of each of the *HST*'s scientific instruments and to see that they are calibrated properly and operated efficiently. There is also a Guide Star Selection System Branch. The telescope's ability to acquire a target and hold it steady depends critically on its fine guidance sensors, which need to lock onto a pair of guide stars in the vicinity of the field under investigation. The Guide Star Branch has responsibility for compiling an all-sky catalog of suitable guide stars from observations using ground-based telescopes. The tasks of the Operations and Data Management Branch are explained by their title—to provide the computing capability to execute the observations and to process and archive the data. The archiving of data (on computer video-disks) so that they can eventually be made freely available to all astronomers is extremely important in the *HST* context. The Research Support and Academic Affairs branches provide broad support for astronomers assigned time on the telescope by the Time Allocation Committee (or requiring assistance in the use of archive data), and will have the very important task of communicating the exciting scientific results from *HST* to the scientific community, to NASA, to Congress, and to the taxpayers (the ultimate patrons of this giant step into the cosmos). There are even more branches for other tasks.

It will take years, perhaps decades, for an informed judgment to be made on the full impact of the *Hubble Space Telescope*. While spectacular new images will reveal objects and phenomena no astronomer has ever dreamed of, the most important science is likely to come from painstaking long-term research programs (many using the archive data). Publicity may initially go to the results from what many astronomers often refer to derogatorily as "hit-and-run astronomy," but the major contributions to science will come from dedicated search and research. It would be a brave person who would gamble on what these major contributions might be; however, it is fun to speculate. Some of the challenges for individual instruments have been described. But what of the long-term goals for *HST*?

A number of the very important questions in astrophysics can be stated quite simply:

How far away are the stars and galaxies? (This is the problem of establishing the "cosmic distance scale.") What is the large-scale structure of the universe? How did the universe begin? How do galaxies evolve? What role do violent events play in the evolution of the universe? How will the universe evolve in the future? (These questions all fall in the realm of cosmology.)

How do the stars and planets form? How do stars evolve and how do they die? What causes activity on the surfaces of the sun and other stars? How widespread is life in the universe? (These are the sciences of stellar and planetary evolution.)

How are the elements formed? How are the elements fused in stellar interiors fed to the interstellar medium to contribute to future generations of stars? What is the role of supernovae and massive stars in forming the heavy elements? (These problems are referred to as nucleogenesis.)

HST will take us a long way toward answering these and other fundamental questions about the cosmos.

Distances in the cosmos are determined via a number of overlapping steps, each step dependent on the preceding one. The more important steps are the following: First one finds the distances to nearby stars using triangulation techniques; the next step is to estimate the distances to nearby star clusters and to study the properties of their variable stars (particularly those called Cepheid variables, whose brightness varies in a periodic way dependent on their intrinsic maximum brightness); Cepheids can then be used to determine the distances to more distant star clusters and indeed to nearby galaxies where Cepheids can be identified; the brightness of the brightest stars in galaxies (and, indeed, supernovae) can also be used to estimate the distances to the nearest galaxies. For more distant galaxies, use is made of the discovery by Hubble that all galaxies are receding from each other and that the more distant a galaxy from the Milky Way the greater its speed of recession (this is Hubble's Law, which can be written in simple equation form as $V = Hd$, where V is recessional speed, d is distance, and H is the so-called Hubble parameter). The speed of recession is determined from the Doppler red shift. Thus, for distant galaxies, red shift is used to estimate distance, albeit with considerable uncertainty.

The critical first step in determining the distance scale is the use of trigonometric parallax for the nearby stars. (This is merely an adaptation of the traditional triangulation technique used by surveyors to determine the distance to remote objects on the earth.) Measurements are taken of the relative position of nearby stars with respect to distant background stars, and then are remeasured six months later, when the earth is on the opposite side of its orbit around the sun, and the difference in apparent positions is determined. The diameter of the earth's orbit is then taken as the baseline to triangulate the distance to the star. From the ground, trigonometric parallax can be used to estimate distances out to about 30 light-years; from *HST* the technique will be applied out to 10 times that distance.

Any errors in the first step of stellar distance determination are carried over and amplified in later steps, so it is critically important to get the first step as accurate as possible. An ESA astrometry spacecraft called *Hipparcos* is due to be launched later in the decade; it will be dedicated to the task of measuring accurately the positions of over 10,000 stars, down to the 9th magnitude, and determining distances from a significant fraction of these. *HST* will determine accurate positions for selected stars down to the 17th magnitude.

Standard distance indicators in external galaxies, such as Cepheids, bright stars, and supernovae, will be investigated in great detail. The use of such calibration objects with *HST* will extend to distances at least 10 times those possible from present ground-based telescopes. (With *HST*, Cepheids can be seen in the galaxies of the nearby Virgo cluster.) Of course, the observations of these calibration objects will also provide important insights into the nature of the objects themselves, independent of their usefulness as distance calibrators.

Astrometry is one of the least glamorous branches of astronomy. It requires very thorough and usually very time-consuming data reduction. However, the results are enormously important, particularly in working toward a refined cosmic distance scale. The complementary observations of *Hipparcos* (of thousands of bright stars) and *HST* (of much fainter objects) will enable us eventually to estimate distances to even the remote extremities of the cosmos with greatly improved precision.

In looking at the large-scale structure of the universe, not only distances are important, but also estimates of the amount of material present. The missing-mass mystery has already been referred to. Quite simply, there does not seem to be enough visible matter in galaxies and clusters of galaxies to explain their dynamic properties. If one looks at the rotation of the stars about the center of a galaxy, the nature of their behavior implies the presence of some 10 times more mass than is visible in stars, gas, and dust in the galaxy. Likewise, the motion of galaxies in clusters suggests that they are gravitationally bound by far more material (again by a factor of 10) than contained in the galaxies themselves. There must be mass there! But no one is certain of the form this hidden mass takes. Possibly it is exotic particles left from the Big Bang; or invisible black holes; or ultralow-mass (Jupiter-type) stars; or . . . ? *HST* alone cannot solve the missing-mass mystery, since observations over the whole of the electromagnetic spectrum will be required. Nevertheless, *HST* can be guaranteed to make an important contribution to the investigation of the problem by searching for low-mass stars, large planets, galactic gaseous halos, intergalactic gas, and evidence for the presence of massive black holes.

Galaxies can be thought of as the basic building blocks of the universe, albeit they tend to swarm in groups, clusters, and super-clusters. Although galaxies appear to come in a bewildering variety of shapes and sizes, it has been suggested that there may be an underlying simplicity in their initial form, with their subsequent evolution (like that of stars) depending strongly on mass. To understand how galaxies evolve, we must study their structure over a wide range of times—from shortly after creation (that is, the most distant, and therefore oldest, galaxies detectable) to their present stage (the nearest galaxies). With the 350-fold increase in the volume of universe accessible to *HST*, it will be possible to study how "normal" galaxies evolve. Of course, there are the "abnormal" galaxies—the quasars, Seyferts, etc. But perhaps it will eventually be shown that they also follow an evolutionary sequence. We can hazard a guess that all active galaxies are powered by massive black holes that grow until they become a quasarlike object when their mass reaches some 100 million solar masses. *HST* observations will probe close to the heart of the quasars and other active galaxies to seek further proof that they are powered by massive black holes and to investigate the various physical processes in their violent activity. There are numerous unanswered questions: What happens to a burned-out quasar? Are quasars related to other active galaxies— and, indeed, normal galaxies? Why does there seem to be a limit to the range of red shifts in which quasars are found? At present we simply do not know the answers to these questions. But if we are ever to find out, the observational power of *HST* can be expected to play an important role. It should enable us to follow, in some detail, the evolution of galaxies from a time when the universe was only 10 percent of its present age.

Statistical studies have revealed that the distribution of galaxies detectable from the ground is rather complex. Although displaying local clustering, groups and clusters appear to be arranged in filamentary structures surrounding giant voids in the universe. However, on the largest scale, the universe does appear generally the same in all directions: It is isotropic. But is the clumping of galaxies evident at the very earliest epochs? *HST* should provide the answer; and only then will scientists be in a position to produce a definitive theory of galaxy formation. At present there are two proposals for galaxy formation. In the isothermal model, small clumps form early in the history of the universe and subsequently aggregate

Formation of galaxies: alternate models

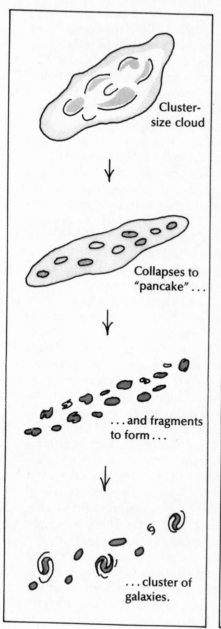

Cluster-size cloud

Collapses to "pancake"...

...and fragments to form...

...cluster of galaxies.

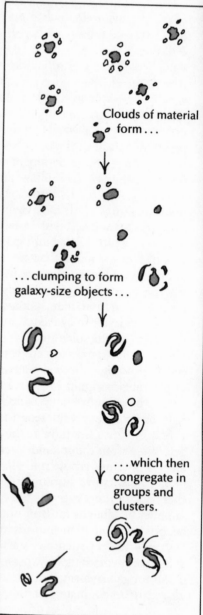

Clouds of material form...

...clumping to form galaxy-size objects...

...which then congregate in groups and clusters.

into galaxies and clusters of galaxies as the universe expands; in the adiabatic model, large structures first appear relatively late in the history of the universe, and galaxies are created in flattened "pancakes" following the gravitational collapse of the larger structures. So, did galaxies evolve from clumps, pancakes, or something else? *HST* should tell us.

The rate of expansion of the universe is described by the Hubble parameter, H. Has the expansion been constant with time? There may be weak evidence for a slowing down of the expansion (described by the so-called deceleration parameter, q), but despite decades of careful observation from the ground, H and q are very poorly determined. There is certainly no consensus among astronomers as to even an approximate value for H: Estimates from different observation techniques differ by a factor of two. It is certain that H, and probably q, will be determined with greatly improved precision from *HST* observations. Only then will we be able to predict whether the expansion of the universe will continue forever, or eventually halt and perhaps even reverse. Do we live in a universe that is gradually running down, or one that goes through stages of growth and regeneration? We are getting closer to solving the ultimate riddle of the cosmos and to reading the mind of the creator. The fundamental importance of the observations in cosmology carried out by *HST* cannot be overemphasized.

Imaging of the planets, moons, and asteroids of our solar system will show surface detail comparable to that revealed on Jupiter during the *Voyager* flyby. However, whereas these probes provided only a fleeting glimpse, the *HST* will enable the planets to be studied over an extended period. Thus astronomers will be able to investigate such phenomena as the complex atmospheric circulation conditions on Jupiter, the intricate ring structure of Saturn, and the wild meteorological conditions of Mars. New moons, asteroids, and comets will be discovered. Ultraviolet observations of comets will prove important in determining the composition of these enigmatic scraps of debris from the primordial solar system. *HST* will enable us to learn much more about both our own planetary system and planetary systems around nearby stars.

As already revealed, probing the birthplace of stars depends on infrared observations, which are beyond the present scope of *HST*. But advances in studying the evolution of stars will be made. A star cluster is the ultimate gold mine for investigating stellar evolution, and *HST* will be able to probe stars at the heart of clusters where detailed observations from the ground are not possible. The very faint members of a cluster population will be studied for the first time. Such investigations will revolutionize our understanding of how stars evolve. An important phase in the evolution of massive stars, and stars in binary systems, occurs during periods of large mass loss. Here the ultraviolet capability of *HST* will prove particularly important.

Of the 400 known radio pulsars, only three have been detected as optical pulsars using ground-based telescopes. The reason for this, quite simply, is that optical pulsars are intrinsically extremely faint and their pulsed emission is difficult to detect against the contamination of the sky's background light. *HST* will discover numerous optical pulsars and optical counterparts of the X-ray sources that eluded detection from the ground because of low brightness. In studying optical pulsars and the optical counterparts of various types of X-ray sources, we have previously been limited by the paucity of data—but no longer.

It is fitting that the mighty Cyclops should have been named after Edwin P. Hubble, who contributed more to our understanding of the cosmos than any other observational astronomer since Galileo. By the time its task is done, probably some three decades or more hence, the *Hubble Space Telescope* will almost certainly have contributed more to our understanding of the cosmos than all previous telescopes combined.

Interlude 5 • Armchair Astronauts

The new generation of space observatories are being designed so that they can be serviced and refurbished in space—a technique successfully demonstrated on space-shuttle missions. But in the future, robots, rather than humans, will play the dominant role. Remotely operated space tugs will shunt spacecraft into appropriate orbits or recover them so that they might be returned to the earth by the shuttle. More spectacularly, free-flying space robots, known in space jargon as teleoperator manipulating systems (TMS), may repair or modify spacecraft in orbit. Any astronomer using a ground-based optical or radio telescope has the freedom to change or modify instruments on his telescope. Space astronomers will one day enjoy comparable flexibility as the space robots set about such tasks. The tragedy of *Challenger* will ensure that robot-development programs will be pursued with urgency, and the role of humans in space should in the future be limited to occasions and activities where their presence is essential.

The technique of telepresence uses a human being, with sensors attached to his or her body, to direct a remote robot to carry out humanlike activities. Thus, if the operator lifted a right arm, the remote robot would do the same. The human operator could see what the robot was "seeing" through a television camera mounted on the robot. By such interaction, it would be possible, for example, for an operator in London to direct an empty car (containing appropriate robotic equipment) through the streets of New York. By turning his head, the operator would cause a camera in the car to rotate and to display the view as if he were actually there; "right-hand down" in London would turn the car to the right in New York; "foot down" in London would produce acceleration in New York, and so on. Exactly the same capability is being planned for robotics in space; ground-based operators could do things in space as if they were actually there. The capabilities of astronauts could be matched, or indeed far exceeded, at least for certain applications. When astronauts leave the shuttle, they have to put on a space suit with complex life-support systems; not so the TMS robots. Astronauts are limited in what they can achieve by the restrictions of their suit, the limited hardware they can transport, the time they can remain active in space, the manipulations they can undertake with just two arms, and so on. Of course, in stressing such limitations, one would not wish to detract from the heroic and exciting exploits of the brave adventurers who have led the way into space. But these explorers would be the first to admit the limitations of humans working in a hostile environment. TMS robots would not be so limited. Humans tire; robots don't. Humans need sleep; robots don't. Humans are limited to the tasks they can perform with two hands; robots could have many. Humans expect vacations and fringe benefits; robots don't (at least not yet!). Telepresence in space is not science fiction, but entirely within the reach of current technology. Armchair astronauts will soon revolutionize the utilization of space, while an army of R2-D2s and C-3POs does the work.

Plans for telepresence involve predictive video displays, which will show what the robot will do before it actually does it. Consider, for example, a telepresence robot carrying out research on the moon. There would be a 2.5-second delay from the time a command was sent by an Earth-based operator until he received confirmation that the command had been executed. With "predictive vision," the operator's display would project the robot's predicted movement 2.5 seconds ahead: A computer would analyze a scene, sense the various directions of any movements, estimate the rate of motion, and hence predict the scene some seconds in the future (subject, of course, to there being no sudden change). Initially, stereo TV cameras will be used, to enable the human operators to see well enough to have a sense of being there. Eventually three-dimensional colored holographic vision will enable operators to look around objects out of reach of the robot.

There are also plans to give the telepresence robots a sense of touch. Handlike devices could match human capabilities and would include force-feedback sensors. Thus when a robot "hand" made contact with an object, it would send a message so that the

A four-armed TMS robot

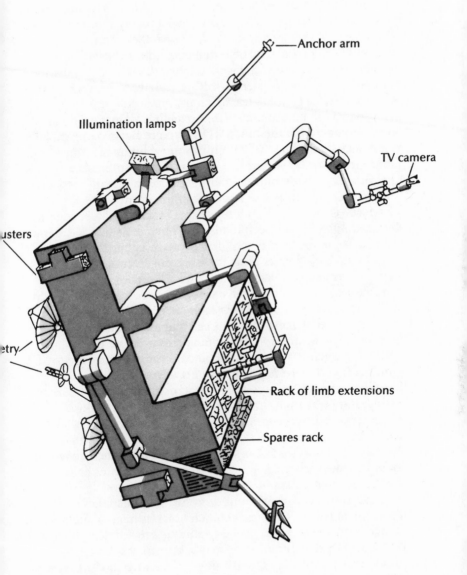

Anchor arm

Illumination lamps

TV camera

usters

etry

Rack of limb extensions

Spares rack

operator could feel the amount of force needed to grip and manipulate the object. Additional sensors could tell whether the object was hot or cold, rough or smooth, of high or low density, perhaps even its composition. Of course, there is no reason why robots should have just two arms. Why not three, four, or more? Multilimbed robots might need several operators. Future-generation telepresence robots will incorporate artificial intelligence, thus dispensing with many of the roles of the earth-based (or shuttle-based) operators. Robots might even eventually service themselves—or at least each other.

It is certain that telepresence robots will play a major role in future exploration of the moon. (Don't forget the amazing exploits of the Soviet Lunokhod robot vehicles in exploring the lunar surface in the early seventies.) Robots will explore the planets and their moons, the asteroids, and the nuclei of comets. The robots will go where humans could never venture.

If many of the long-term future needs of space will depend on the capabilities of high-tech robots, the immediate future depends on the need to reestablish confidence in conventional launchers. The shuttle incorporates what, by space-engineering standards, is well tried technology; yet unnecessary risk taking, unsatisfactory communication, and unwieldy management led to an avoidable tragedy. Some confidence might have been rapidly restored if NASA's arsenal of aging conventional launchers could have kept a U.S. presence in space while the problems with the shuttle (and NASA management) were sorted out. Instead, a nation rightly proud of its advanced technological prowess suffered the humiliation of seeing once-reliable rockets fail one after another. European expectations that their Ariane launcher could gain commercial advantage through NASA's problems proved short-lived. An Ariane failure followed on the heels of the losses of NASA's Titan and Delta launchers. So what had gone wrong with Western space technology? Loss of technical expertise? Sabotage? Or just plain bad luck?

Lack of technical expertise is certainly not a reason. Titan, Delta, and even the *Challenger* booster rockets represent reasonably straightforward technology (albeit with uncorrected design faults in the case of *Challenger*). The aging workhorse rockets, Titan and Delta, may have suffered from being at the end of production runs, NASA having unwisely placed almost all their eggs in the shuttle basket. Nor can the idea of sabotage seriously be entertained. Security in the space game is extremely tight and effective. So we come back to a run of extremely bad luck. There will always be a significant risk element in aviation, yet modern aircraft have an impressive safety record, and the risks are deemed acceptable. Rockets are more uncertain beasts. Even with all the precautions, with all the commitment, with all the quality-control procedures, with the investment of vast sums of money, the possibility of failure will always be there. Risk analysis may show that the risk of failure is small but nevertheless present. Perhaps one of NASA's most serious failures was to present a picture of reliability and low risk that could never be achieved. After almost 20 years of grand successes and spectacular achievement, perhaps they had unwittingly started to believe in their own infallibility. Those who understand the real scope of the technological achievements in space are saddened to see a mighty agency humbled. The Western nations will reestablish their position of competence in rocketry; it is an urgent need, for science, for commerce, and for military security. But claims that a "state of emergency" existed for the Western world following recent space failures were exaggerated and premature.

Is there a long-term role for humans in space? That is a question many have asked since the beginning of the Space Age. If the Soviet Union had not launched a man into space (motivated by a desire for political prestige and to demonstrate technical superiority, rather than for scientific need) would the United States have opted for a manned program? If there had been no Cold War and no arms race, then would there have been a moon race? Why has it been only the superpowers that have found it necessary to have manned space missions, while Europe, Japan, and other countries have maintained advanced space science and applications programs (at a small fraction of the cost) without? (Actually, Europe has had a manned space module, called *Spacelab*, mounted in the shuttle and has provisional plans for a minishuttle.) More considered thought should have been given to the role of humans in space. Adventure is, of course, an admirable endeavor; it is in our nature to explore the unknown. One must greatly admire the brave young (and now not so young) men and women who volunteer for space service, attracted by the challenge and the spirit of adventure. Certain space activities have clearly benefited from the human presence—for example, biomedical research. And the science of robotics was not far enough advanced to perform the tasks demanded of humans in space activities to date, although the technology could have been accelerated had the decision been made to rely on machines rather than to risk human lives.

Men and women will continue to venture into space. The challenge for the human species to explore the unknown and to push human capabilities to the limit is too great to opt out now. Besides, why should robots inherit the cosmos? But the risks will always be high, and space adventure must be limited to those who really understand the risks and are trained to take them. So please, Mr. President, Senator, or NASA administrator, no more citizens in space, no more politicians in space, and no more teachers in space! Let's stop all this nonsense of "tourists" in space. Space is for the professionals. Robots in space, fine. Amateurs in space, never again!

In the future, the real reason for humans in space, and the real risks involved, should be made clear to the tolerant taxpayers who finance space adventure. Most scientists would be happy with an obedient R2-D2 and an ambidextrous C-3PO.

── 6 ──
TEMPLES TO THE GODS

ASTRONOMERS ARE ALREADY DREAMING OF ORBITING TELE-scopes very much larger than the *Hubble Space Telescope*. Okay, so *HST* can view 350 times the volume of the universe observable with a ground-based telescope, but there is plenty more to see beyond that. Imagine the observable universe scaled to the size of a giant balloon, 1 kilometer in radius. The Milky Way would be the size of a dime somewhere within the balloon. A nearby galaxy would be another dime about a meter away, and a nearby cluster of galaxies would be at a distance of a few tens of meters. The universe accessible to *HST* would still encompass only a small fraction of the volume of the balloon. But can we look even further back toward the creation? Can we detect faint objects beyond the power of *HST*? Can we hope to see greater detail than even *HST* can resolve?

There can be no doubt that *HST* represents the ultimate in conventional telescopes of its size. Could one ever justify the enormous cost of constructing a conventional space telescope of, say, 5 meters' aperture? Its sheer size and weight would require a "super-shuttle" to launch it, and the cost of such a space observatory would be measured in tens of billions of dollars. No, science, let alone political posturing, could never justify an expenditure on such a scale for the next generation space telescope. If space telescopes are to get bigger, then we will need to investigate alternative technologies capable of producing giant structures at comparatively low cost. One possibility is to use segmented mirrors; a large structure could then be assembled in space from precision segments launched in "kit" form. An example of this concept is the so-called *Large Deployable Reflector* (LDR), presently envisaged for far-infrared wavelengths, which might cope with reflector diameters of up to 20 meters. Dreaming of even larger structures gave birth to the concept of a *Vast Orbiting Reflector* (VOR). (Vor was an all-seeing Norse goddess.)

In a reflecting telescope, the essential elements are, of course, the mirror surfaces. The rest of the telescope is a structure to support the carefully figured reflecting surfaces and to sustain their shape. But in space, there could be alternative ways of achieving and sustaining the accurate shape required for the mirrors. It has been proposed that mirrors could be made from extremely thin films of durable organic polymer stowed in a shuttle cargo bay, and inflated, or shaped, in orbit. With a film thickness of 25 microns, a 100-meter-diameter film "mirror" could be constructed in orbit that would weigh the same as the *HST* primary mirror. Just how an inflated thin-film telescope could be figured in space remains mere speculation; vacuum shaping is a technique tried on the ground, for small structures, with some success. But there would obviously be enormous problems; for example, how would one isolate a segment of the structure perforated by a micrometeorite? Could the inflatable optical system be manufactured, stowed, launched, and then inflated in orbit to achieve an acceptable standard of accuracy at, say, far-infrared wavelengths, let alone at optical wavelengths?

Use of inflated structures in space is not new: The *Echo* telecommunications satellites, which fascinated sky watchers of the sixties, were balloons fabricated from polyester film. But the *Echo* "satelloons" (as they became known) did not need to meet the exceptional optical precision of a VOR.

The new technologies required for giant mirrors in space might well evolve as part of the research for the Strategic Defense Initiative. If they do, astronomers will be ready, willing, and able to turn them to good scientific use. At the moment, giant space telescopes are but a distant dream—but 40 years ago, so was *HST*.

The objective of an *LDR* or a *VOR* is to collect more radiation. The light-gathering capacity of a telescope depends on the area of its aperture. Thus a 2-meter-diameter telescope gathers four times the light of a 1-meter telescope; a 100-meter telescope would gather 1,500 times more light than a 2.4-meter space telescope (the size of *HST*). And so on. So if it is extremely faint objects you are after, you need large mirror size—even from space. If it is vastly improved angular resolution you are after, however, then this can be achieved using telescopes of more modest size. Note the plural —telescopes! Improved angular resolution can be achieved by using an array of small telescopes connected to form what is called an interferometer.

Interferometers have been used with enormous success in ground-based radio astronomy. The resolution of a conventional telescope (that is, its ability to resolve fine detail) at a particular wavelength depends on the telescope aperture: The larger the telescope, the greater the detail it can resolve. The trick in interferometry is to mimic the effect of a large aperture by using small-aperture telescopes. Thus, for example, an array of radio telescopes whose outer elements are separated by, say, 5 kilometers, would have a resolution comparable to that of a giant telescope with an aperture of 5 kilometers. The rotation of the earth is used to synthesize the complete aperture. Of course, the array of small telescopes can't collect as much radiation as the mimicked giant telescope, but it does achieve the same resolution. Very-long-baseline interferometry (VLBI) using radio telescopes separated by thousands of kilometers (sometimes involving intercontinental linkups), has been used to achieve spectacular resolutions. The resolving power of VLBI networks at radio wavelengths already exceeds that possible from *HST* for optical wavelengths by a hundredfold.

Radio astronomers would like to improve the potential of interferometry by placing a radio telescope in space linked to ground-based radio-telescope networks. The space-borne telescope could be placed in an elliptical orbit, with an apogee (that is, furthest point from the earth) of about 20,000 kilometers—thus achieving unprecedented resolution, some 50 times better than that possible using ground-based networks alone. By combining the space and ground data, one effectively simulates a radio telescope with a diameter of some 25,000 kilometers! ESA and NASA have been studying the possibility of deploying such a radio telescope in space, called *QUASAT*, to be used in unison with ground-based radio-linked radio telescopes. The resolution capability of *QUASAT* would be comparable to resolving a postage stamp on the moon. *QUASAT* will probe the heart of the quasars, to a scale of less than a light-day.

The linking of ground-based optical telescopes to form an optical interferometer is a relatively recent achievement. The task of developing the instrumentation necessary to convert incoming light to electrical signals that can be combined and processed to achieve extreme resolution has not been an easy one. However, once this advanced technology has been mastered on the ground, it will be only a matter of time before the added advantages of space interferometry will be realized. Within the next few decades, small space telescopes flying in formation will mimic the precision and extreme resolution of a mighty space telescope. Then it will be possible to "see" the surface detail of nearby stars and their planetary systems in a way that is now possible only for the sun and planets of the solar system, to resolve individual stars in even distant galaxies in a way that is now possible only for relatively nearby galaxies, and to probe the very heart of the distant quasars in optical light in a way that is now possible only with radio interferometry. The price will be high but not beyond the bounds of projected space-science funding; in this case the potential scientific gains will undoubtedly justify the cost.

The immediate future of optical astronomy from space is secure with the *Hubble Space Telescope*, so it needs to be stressed that large segmented space telescopes or space optical-interferometry missions are unlikely to be in place in this century. However, plans for the next generation of X-ray observatories are now well advanced.

NASA's *AXAF*, the *Advanced X-Ray Astronomical Facility*, should be thought of as the X-ray equivalent of *HST*—a giant space observatory planned to be in orbit for decades, but with the potential for regular refurbishment and interchange of instruments in space and, if necessary, for return to Earth for major repairs.

AXAF will comprise a nest of grazing-incidence X-ray telescopes of outer diameter 1.2 meters. It will achieve a hundredfold increase in sensitivity over the *Einstein Observatory*. It will point with extreme precision and will achieve 0.5-arc-second resolution —comparable to the very best ground-based optical telescope. *AXAF* will equal, or perhaps even exceed, the *HST* in its ability to study distant clusters of galaxies and quasars.

Just when *AXAF* goes into orbit depends on financial rather than technological or scientific constraints. Most of the technology required for the mission exists, or is under development. It will incorporate many systems similar to *HST* and will be operated by an institute resembling the Space Telescope Science Institute. The first generation of instruments will be capable of high-resolution imaging, spectroscopy, and polarimetry. A modular design will enable instruments to be replaced every few years, so that up-to-date technologies can be incorporated.

AXAF

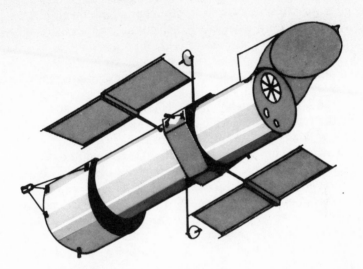

Various other, smaller X-ray satellites will be launched, dedicated to tasks that will complement or supplement the capabilities of AXAF. For example, the *X-Ray Transient Explorer* (XTE) will study compact galactic X-ray sources to investigate the way their output varies with time. It is known that the nature of the X rays from interacting binary systems is highly variable; *XTE* will study the mechanisms of X-ray bursts and other transient phenomena. But perhaps the future X-ray mission with the greatest potential significance is in the area of spectroscopy. The X-ray emission spectrum from hot gaseous systems, such as stellar coronae, supernova remnants, hot interstellar material, the galactic halo, and intergalactic gas, is rich in astrophysically important information. For spectroscopy, one principally needs to collect the maximum possible radiation; what is needed is high "throughput," while spatial resolution is not so important. When as much radiation as possible is gathered, it can then be dispersed into its component "colors" in a spectrum. Thus the requirements of a high-through-put spectroscopy mission are not exactly those of a mission like AXAF. Of course, AXAF will have spectrographs among its instrument complement, but the performance of the AXAF telescope will be optimized for imaging, and more spacecraft time is likely to be given over to this than to spectroscopy. Consequently X-ray astronomers yearn for a dedicated high-throughput spectroscopy mission. This is likely to use novel X-ray telescope configurations that will maximize the amount of X radiation focused onto an X-ray spectrometer, although such a new instrument may have somewhat inferior spatial resolution compared to the precision X-ray telescopes of AXAF, Einstein, and ROSAT.

By the turn of the century, X-ray astronomers will have access to a powerful armory—AXAF, a high-throughput spectroscopy instrument, and small mission-oriented X-ray satellites. The potential scientific yield from the X-ray sky remains extremely high.

Gamma rays from the cosmos are important, but to date they have been rather poorly studied. In the terrestrial environment, they are synonymous with nuclear radioactivity—both natural and man-made. Gamma rays are very energetic and can penetrate several centimeters of lead. Their effect on living cells can be deadly, as has been horrifically demonstrated in the victims of the atom bombs and of nuclear accidents. All except the very-highest-energy gamma rays from space are stopped from reaching the earth's surface by the atmosphere, but they have been detected by experiments on high-altitude balloons and on satellites.

Gamma rays cannot be focused to form images and can be detected only indirectly, by their interaction with matter in the detector. For example, one type of detector utilizes pulses of light they produce in certain plastic and crystalline materials called scintillators. Another detection technique utilizes the electron-positron pair created when a gamma ray interacts with matter. (A positron is a fundamental particle with mass identical to that of an electron but with positive charge.) Since cosmic gamma rays are rather sparse and can't be focused, detectors need to be large if they are to have acceptable sensitivity. Because of their extremely short wavelength, we do not characterize gamma rays with the common terms *wavelength* or *frequency*; rather, we use an equivalent measure—energy. The unit of energy used is the electron volt. In such energy terms, visible light is equivalent to approximately 1 electron volt; gamma rays start at energies of 100,000 electron volts! We don't know how far they extend, but they have been detected to energies of billions of electron volts. The range of energies of gamma rays is more than 10,000 times the range for visible light and more than 100 times the range for X rays. It is an enormously important part of the electromagnetic spectrum, only poorly exploited so far by astronomers.

Only about 30 cosmic gamma-ray sources are known, most of which were discovered by an ESA spacecraft called COS-B and a NASA satellite called SAS-2; among these are the Crab pulsar, the famous quasar 3C273, the X-ray binary Cygnus X-3, and gamma-ray "hot spots" attributed to energetic cosmic rays colliding with matter in dense interstellar clouds. However, the resolution and sensitivity of the COS-B and SAS-2 gamma-ray detectors were low. The Los Alamos hydrogen-bomb scientists put a network of gamma-ray detectors in orbit on the Vela satellites, to search for atmospheric explosions breaking the Nuclear Test-Ban Treaty. Astronomers were startled to learn that these satellites were detecting sudden bursts of gamma radiation from outside the solar system. Several bursts per year were being detected, and by comparing data from different spacecraft, scientists could determine the direction in the sky from which the radiation originated. A very bright burst source, which could give important clues to their origin, occurred on March 5, 1979. Its position could be determined with some accuracy and coincided with a supernova remnant called N49, in the large Magellanic Cloud, a satellite galaxy to the Milky Way. If, as seems likely, the burst source is associated with the supernova remnant, the most probable link is a neutron star at the remnant's center. Perhaps gamma-ray bursts are due to giant nuclear explosions occurring on the surfaces of neutron stars. The magnitude of these massive bursts needs to be emphasized: They release more energy in 0.1 seconds than our sun releases in 10,000 years!

Because of the poor resolution of the COS-B and SAS-2 detectors, few gamma-ray sources have been located with sufficient accuracy to identify the star systems producing the gamma rays. Obviously the Crab pulsar and Cygnus X-3 are exceptions. There is an intriguing object in Gemini, dubbed Geminga, where associated X-ray emission detected by the *Einstein Observatory* enabled the position to be determined with extreme accuracy; there is a very faint star near the position, but it is uncertain whether it represents the underlying object. Geminga is the first cosmic object discovered solely from its gamma-ray emission.

Gamma-ray astronomy could provide unique information on the mechanisms of pulsar radiation, the distribution of cosmic rays in the galaxy, and the ultra-energetic processes at the centers of active galaxies. The years of neglect of this very important discipline will end when NASA launches its *Gamma Ray Observatory* (GRO) in the early 1990s. The sensitivity of the GRO detectors will surpass those of previous missions by a factor of more than 10 and will have substantially better resolution as well.

The observatory will include an instrument specifically designed to study the enigmatic gamma-ray burst sources. The "burst and transient source experiment" will monitor the whole sky (except that portion occulted at any time by the earth) for gamma-ray bursts or other short-duration phenomena. A low-energy instrument will do spectroscopy from 100,000 to 10 million electron volts; a mid-range instrument will operate from 1 to 30 million electron volts; and the highest energy range will be covered by an instrument working from 20 million to 30 billion electron volts. Note the overlap between the instruments. Gamma-ray astronomy of worthwhile sensitivity requires big instruments; the GRO instruments will weigh some 6 tons and the full observatory will weigh 15 tons.

GRO will allow the long-neglected gamma-ray astronomers to enjoy some of the benefits that in the past have been so lavishly afforded to those working in other space-astronomy disciplines.

In following up the highly successful *Infrared Astronomical Satellite* (IRAS) mission, European astronomers have taken a lead over their U.S. colleagues. ESA has selected the *Infrared Space Observatory* (ISO) as their next major space-astronomy mission. ISO is a natural successor to IRAS. IRAS was an exploratory mission to survey the infrared sky and to catalog the multitude of infrared sources detected. Now comes the detailed science—the high-resolution imaging, the photometry, the spectroscopy, and the polarimetry. IRAS gave some hint of the enormous wealth of exciting astronomy awaiting the development of a high-sensitivity infrared observatory. Again, a telescope in Earth orbit, cooled to within a few degrees of absolute zero, is needed to fully exploit the technologies for infrared detection. ISO will, like IRAS, be based on a 0.6-meter-diameter telescope cooled by a cryogen system involving 100 kilograms of superfluid helium and 50 kilograms of liquid hy-

ESA's *Infrared Space Observatory*

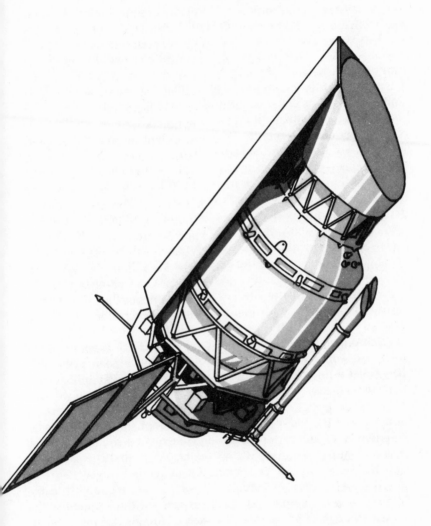

drogen. The system should provide about two years of cooled operation. At the focus of the telescope there will be four instruments—a camera, a photometer/polarimeter, and two spectrometers, covering long and short infrared wavelengths.

NASA sees the next step in infrared astronomy as the *Shuttle Infrared Telescope Facility* (*SIRTF*). *SIRTF* requires dedicated shuttle flights, since the telescope and instruments will fill the cargo bay; it is a very much larger system than envisaged for *ISO*. Initially *SIRTF* is designed for multiple shuttle flights, of from 7 to 14 days each; eventually it might be let loose from the shuttle to fly free for periods of 6 months or more, to then be recovered, refurbished, and its cryogenic supply of liquid helium "topped up." For early flights, only two instruments will be mounted on the telescope, although this will be increased to a full complement of six instruments, including a high-sensitivity photometer, long-wavelength and short-wavelength cameras, and spectrographs with one dedicated to the study of very faint objects.

NASA's intermediate-term vision for space astronomy is based on its large orbiting observatories covering most of the electromagnetic spectrum—GRO for gamma rays, AXAF for X rays, HST for ultraviolet and optical, and SIRTF for infrared. ESA's intermediate-term vision for astronomy is focused on a plan known as Horizon 2000. For cosmic astronomy this includes two major missions, a high-throughput spectroscopy mission for X-ray astronomy and a telescope working in the far infrared (at wavelengths intermediate between the infrared and microwaves). Missions of more modest scale will embrace the far ultraviolet (*Lyman*) and infrared (*ISO*).

Immediately beyond the plans for the next generation of space observatories lies the specter of the space station. U.S. proposals for a permanently manned space station have divided the international space-science community. Its opponents argue that the space station has little to do with science but rather is being dictated by global power politics. Because the Soviets are developing the capability for a large permanently manned space station, some feel the United States and its allies must match or surpass it. Proponents of the space station argue that it will enable spacecraft to be refurbished in orbit and giant astronomical facilities to be assembled in space, and it could be used as a launch base for missions to the planets. The space station is romantically envisaged as a beachhead on the new "continent" of space.

One of the most respected U.S. space scientists since the dawn of the satellite era has been James A. Van Allen, after whom the radiation belts girding the earth are named. Van Allen is a strong critic of the space station. He has written:

> There is something about the topic of outer space that induces hyperbolic expectation. With no difficulty at all I can think of a billion-dollar space mission before breakfast any day of the week and a multibillion-dollar mission on Sunday. Ordinarily I do not inflict such visions on my fellow citizens, but I note that proposals of comparable or lesser merit and of much greater cost receive public attention, and some are influential in high circles of government. I submit that the proposed permanently manned space station is in this category. . . . The progressive loss of U.S. leadership in space science can be attributed, I believe, largely to our excessive emphasis on manned space flight and on vaguely perceived, poorly founded goals of a highly speculative nature. Given the current budgetary climate and a roughly constant level of public support for civil space ventures, the development of a space station, if pursued as now projected, will seriously reduce the opportunities for advances in space science and in important applications of space technology in the coming decade.

Powerful stuff!

Like Van Allen, many space scientists are convinced that scientific objectives can be realized more cheaply, and with greater flexibility, by robot spacecraft. Maybe. But one would be naive to forget the international connotations of the moon race, the perceived military importance of space, the need to set national technical challenges. It is true that two-thirds of NASA's budget has gone to its manned programs (principally Apollo and the shuttle). But it is not obvious that without the political, military, technical, and adventure aspects of the manned programs Congress would have made these funds available to space science using robot spacecraft.

NASA's dream of a space station is a longstanding one. After Apollo, it needed a large, prestigious project. It wanted the shuttle and the space station; it got the shuttle. After the shuttle, it reset its sights on the space station. In May 1982, NASA created an internal task force to undertake studies on the concept. The objectives of the space station were to:

Establish a means for the permanent presence of people in space

Provide a capability for routine, continuous utilization of space, for science, technology, industry, national security, and general operations

Lead to the development and exploitation of the synergistic effects of the man/machine combination in space

Provide for essential system elements and operational practices for an integrated national space capability

Reduce the cost and complexity of living in and using space

NASA believed these objectives could be met by building on a relatively modest core facility to be in orbit by 1992. This would be built in orbit by parts ferried up by the shuttle fleet. First there would be a central module, and later flights would add truss structures, solar arrays, habitat modules, laboratories, and service modules. Compared with earlier generations of orbiting facilities (such as *Skylab* and the Soviet *Salyut* space station), astronauts could live in less spartan conditions. The habitat modules would provide living quarters, offices, and a gymnasium and sick bay. Additional modules could be added over time to provide an expanded and enhanced facility. The core facility would provide an initial operations capability (IOC). It would house six to eight people, several laboratories, and a workshop for repairing payloads recovered from orbit. Provision would be made on the station for the external attachment of instruments for Earth-oriented and astronomical observations. In addition, unmanned platforms would be provided—one in an orbit similar to the space station's (and which could be serviced from the station) and one in a polar orbit. An orbit maneuvering vehicle (OMV) would carry orbiting spacecraft to and from the space station. Later an orbit transfer vehicle (OTV) would be capable of transferring equipment to and from geostationary orbit. The space station would serve as an experiment platform, a control and data center for space missions, a service center for satellites requiring refurbishment and repair, an assembly base for construction and deployment of giant experiments, and a support node for unmanned platforms. There were unstated military requirements. All this was hardly "Buck Rogers" or "Star Trek," but a relatively modest step toward a permanently manned presence in space.

NASA asked the Space Sciences Board of the National Academy of Science to look at how the space station could serve the needs of science. The NAS started a year-long study in September 1982. If NASA had hoped for strong support from scientists, they were to be disappointed. The NAS report concluded:

> The Board examined the set of specific missions proposed for implementation from the space station system during the years 1991–2000. It has found that few of these missions would acquire significant scientific or technical enhancement by virtue of being implemented from this space station. In view of this and the adequacy of the present space transportation system for the purposes of space science, the Board sees no scientific need for this space station during the next twenty years.

However, the board did state that if it was decided to proceed with the space station for reasons associated with national policy, then they would work with NASA to enhance its scientific potential. But by now the future for the space station was to be determined by political lobbying on Capitol Hill and by debates on defense strategy and national policy issues. The voice of science, if not silenced, was at least ignored temporarily.

In January 1984, President Reagan announced during his State of the Union address that he had given directions to NASA to proceed with the development of the space station. Congressional approval was given for a two-year detailed design study. International partners were sought and obtained; Europe, Japan, and Canada agreed to consider joining the mission.

If many scientists were lukewarm in their support for the space station, it was nevertheless very important for NASA (and its new international partners) to obtain direction from scientists in defining the requirements for the station. In January 1984, NASA created a Task Force on Scientific Uses of Space Station to provide such direction.

No one would pretend that the space station is an ideal platform for astronomical observations. The accurate pointing of telescopes requires that they be free of vibrations, but an astronaut's sneeze would be sufficient to disturb a precision pointing system. Astronomy from space requires the best possible observation conditions; one needs to know that instruments are free from contamination,

Space station

To the coorbiting
unmanned platform

To geostationary orbit

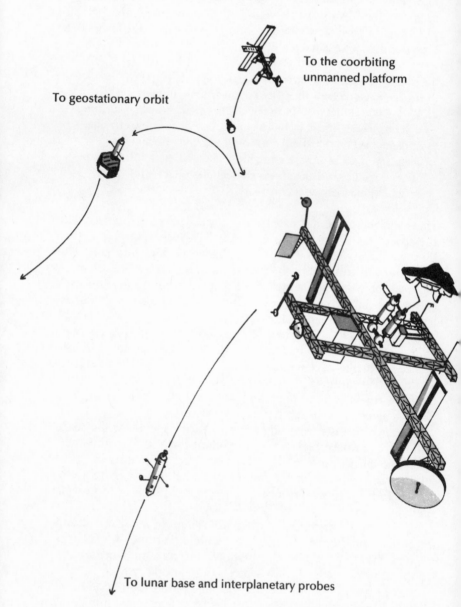

To lunar base and interplanetary probes

but clouds of gas from thrusters and the discharge of waste will mean that the space-station environment will be "dirty." Sensitive instruments must be free from interference, but the space station will be "noisy." Yet when the Task Force on Scientific Uses of Space Station convened at Stanford University in August 1984 for a one-week study, it met under a banner proclaiming: "Space station is approved and going ahead; how can science use it and, indeed, help to design it?"

The space station must have some things to offer for science, surely. If it were to be of real use for astronomical research, then the astronomers were intent on laying down a few conditions:

Missions should be based solely on scientific goals and priorities (as established by scientists, not politicians or administrators).

There must be unmanned, small (single-mission) coorbiting platforms, free from the contamination and interference of the manned station.

Provision must be made for the assembly, deployment, and check-out of large facilities, up to 50 meters in diameter.

More money must be made available immediately to develop instrumentation and expertise (using rockets and shuttle payloads), leading up to the space station.

International collaboration on experiments should be encouraged at all levels.

Technical requirements should be determined in consultation with scientists, and interfaces and documentation should be kept simple.

If these requirements could be met, then at least some astronomers were prepared to admit that the advent of the space-station era might have something to offer to astronomy. The most important new capability was felt to be the use of the space station for routine maintenance, upgrade, and repair of facilities in orbit. Discovery keeps pace with advances in technology. The space station could enable the periodic upgrade of space facilities as new technological breakthroughs are made. The mighty space observatories HST, AXAF, GRO, and SIRTF could be serviced routinely in orbit. The robot OMV would capture a spacecraft and bring it to a service hangar, where astronauts could work on it in a "shirtsleeve" environment. More modest instruments could be mounted on smaller coorbiting platforms. It was also realized that the space station would be important for the assembly of giant structures launched in an unassembled packaged configuration. An assembly area would be needed to unpack components, join them together, mate the structure with instruments, and check out the whole system before its release as a free-flying observatory. The *LDR* has already been mentioned as a prospective mission of this type. Ultralarge, deployable experiments have also been proposed for cosmic-ray and gamma-ray astronomy. And space-interferometry optical arrays also lend themselves to assembly and deployment in orbit. Already there are plans for a *Coherent Optical System of Modular Imaging Collectors* (COSMIC), a modular interferometer array with milli-arc-second resolution, to be assembled in orbit.

Some astronomers have acknowledged that the manned space station could accommodate large experiments where stable pointing and contamination were not constraints—for example, cosmic-ray research. Also, there could be certain experiments where the presence of human observers might be beneficial—for example, in solar astronomy. And the space station is recognized as providing a useful assembly and staging post for interplanetary spacecraft.

There are groups of scientists, other than astronomers, who do seem genuinely enthusiastic about the space station—for example, those who would benefit from a microgravity environment for research in materials and the life sciences. Perhaps the majority of astronomers are naturally of a rather conservative nature. Certainly their training ensures that they question even the apparently obvious. Time will tell whether the concerns expressed about the space station are justified. But we must acknowledge that the great space-station debate has been divisive for science. Could the aspirations of scientists be better and more cheaply served by robot spacecraft? Should we be putting so much money into manned missions when the bulk of space science does not need a human presence? Isn't a permanently manned space station really about political posturing and military adventurism? Perhaps the last word on these points should be from James Van Allen:

The acceptance of such grandiose proposals [as the space station] by otherwise rational individuals stems from the mystique of space flight, as nurtured over many centuries by early writers of science fiction and their present-day counterparts. Indeed, to the ordinary person space flight is synonymous with the flight of human beings.

The simple taste for adventure and fantasy expressed in that sentiment has been elevated in some quarters to the quasi-religious belief that space is a natural habitat of human beings. According to this belief, the real goal of the space program is to establish "man's permanent presence in space," a slogan that does not respond to the simple question: "For what purpose?" . . . In the more than 28 years since the launching of *Sputnik 1*, the overwhelming majority of scientific and utilitarian achievements in space have come from unmanned, automated, and commandable spacecraft.

Let's imagine that we are reviewing the state of space astronomy in the year 2000. Gamma-ray astronomy will have been revolutionized by the GRO mission; at last this important branch of astrophysics will have come into its own. Although the pioneering COS-B and SAS-2 missions had made a few tens of gamma-ray discoveries, GRO will have made thousands. There will be pulsars, active galaxies, interacting binaries, and the enigmatic bursters. Already GRO will have had a major servicing and upgrade in orbit, using the space-station facilities. Minor repairs and instrument changes will have been completed on the station using robot devices. But since larger gamma-ray detectors have greater sensitivity, a major new gamma-ray facility will be mated to the space station. It is called the *Gamma Ray Imaging Tank System* (GRITS), and the detecting medium will be gas in a giant container; indeed, the container to be exploited is the external fuel tank of a shuttle. Astronauts and robot craft will modify the expended tank to fit detectors, optics, electronics, and gas, to convert it into a mighty gamma-ray telescope capable of taking the next major step forward in gamma-ray astronomy.

By the year 2000 X-ray astronomy will be exploiting the complementary activities of AXAF and a high-throughput spectroscopy mission. The enormous promise of X-ray astronomy, realized in the seventies and eighties, will at last be coming to fruition. Here is the astronomer's eye on the violent universe—the superenergetic and turbulent systems at the heart of galaxies, in stellar explosions, in the hot gas between the stars and between the galaxies. But the power of the X-ray eye will be limited by the size of the telescopes. Again the cry is for bigger and better. The turn of the century will see plans well advanced for a 5-meter-class X-ray space observatory, assembled in space on the space station, to be set free on a coorbiting platform. And the advanced technology to exploit X-ray interferometry will be under investigation, to achieve X-ray images of milli-arc-second resolution.

In the far ultraviolet, the *Lyman* mission will have been hailed as a major breakthrough. The richness of the far-ultraviolet spectrum means that it must be fully exploited, if we are to gain a full understanding of the physics and chemistry of astronomical systems displaying temperatures of tens of thousands of degrees. *Lyman* will have cracked the deuterium problem for the Milky Way and for a few nearby galaxies. But we will need to probe deeper into the cosmos to convince ourselves that we really understand the chemical evolution of the universe. A *Super Lyman* will be needed, the size of *HST*, but exploiting and enhancing the new far-ultraviolet technologies pioneered on *Lyman*.

In the optical region, *HST* will by the year 2000 have surpassed even the most optimistic expectations; mighty Cyclops will have revolutionized our understanding of all previously known astrophysical systems and phenomena, as well as discovering previously unknown and totally unexpected types of objects. It will have been regularly refurbished in orbit, with new instruments fitted to exploit state-of-the-art technology. Plans will be in hand for a new segmented telescope of at least 10-meter-equivalent diameter. But there is a limit to the usefulness of an optical telescope, regardless of size, in Earth orbit: The zodiacal light still produces a background sky brightness, masking the very faintest objects from view. The dust (probably from comets) that scatters sunlight to produce the zodiacal light is concentrated in the ecliptic plane (the plane in which the planets orbit the sun). So the plan will be to send the new 10-meter space telescope into a deep-space orbit, out of the ecliptic, thus escaping from the final significant source of background light contamination. The COSMIC interferometer array will now be in orbit, having been assembled, aligned, and tested from the space station; eventually the interferometer array will be extended to improve its resolving power further. Then nearby red giants will be seen in detail comparable to naked-eye observations of the moon; planetary systems around nearby stars will also be visible.

At the century's turn, infrared astronomy will be benefiting from the advent of the space station. *SIRTF* will have been regularly serviced (at six-month intervals) from the space station to have its cryogenic system replenished. The ability to regularly replenish cryostats from the space station will mean that plans for a 5-meter-class infrared space telescope will be perfectly viable. So will be plans for an infrared interferometric array. At long last, the far-infrared region will be fully exploited, with a *Large Deployable Reflector* constructed and serviced from the space station.

Following the success of *QUASAT*, radio interferometry will be further enhanced by putting a space radio telescope into a deep-space orbit, extending the baseline to millions of kilometers. Now the centers of the radio quasar will be probed to a scale of a few light-hours—that is, of a dimension similar to that of our solar system.

It is not too difficult to envisage the type of technical advances that might be made over the next 10 to 20 years that will shape the next generation of space observatories. By the year 2000, astronomers will be exploiting the space observatories already under development, or at least being talked about. The space station and space robots will be the foundations for the new missions. It is rather more speculative to look beyond that point, to, say, the year 2050. What might then be offered?

By 2050 (probably, in fact, well before) there will be space stations in geostationary orbit. This orbit has many attractions: It is in permanent line-of-sight contact with ground stations; it is a low-energy staging point for deep space probes; and it allows long, uninterrupted observations of the heavens. Other attractive sites for space stations are the so-called earth-moon Lagrangian point (the position where the gravitational attraction of the earth and the moon are equal) and the earth-sun Lagrangian point.

Men and women will be back on the moon by 2050, now in large (thousand-member) scientific colonies. Mining operations will have been initiated. Gaseous oxygen production will be possible for life support and to make liquid oxygen for fueling Earth-bound and deep-space-bound rockets. Closed ecological systems will be under development. Mining will have led to metal extraction for construction materials. Rapid, reliable transportation will be available from the lunar base throughout the solar system. Manned missions will have explored the surface of Mars and several of the satellites of Jupiter. Unmanned "rover" missions will have wandered the surfaces of Mercury and Venus and the atmospheres of Jupiter and Saturn. Robot probes will have been on sample-return missions to asteroids, cometary nuclei, and the outer planets. By now the artificial intelligence of robots will be approaching that of humans. The first unmanned interstellar probe will be on the drawing board, but manned interstellar probes will still be a century or two away. Speculation? Yes. Fantasy? No.

What will the twenty-first-century space capabilities mean for astronomy? Well, what space astronomers need is a large, *stable*, platform in Earth orbit on which to build their instruments and facilities. It must be free from contamination and interference. It must be easily serviced and allow long periods of uninterrupted observation. It must be large enough for the construction and deployment of astronomical facilities of ever-increasing size and complexity. Such a large, stable platform already exists in Earth orbit—the moon. It seems almost certain that permanently manned lunar observatories will be in place in the twenty-first century, perhaps as early as 2010, but certainly by 2020. By 2050 these observatories will be of an advanced nature, the ideal sites for major astronomical research facilities.

What will be the situation by 2100? Stellar probes? Space colonies? Looking that far ahead, the crystal ball and the brain become hazy. Speculation starts to merge with fantasy.

EPILOGUE
Mission of Hermes

Hermes was the son of Zeus. He is represented as the messenger of the gods and as the god of science, commerce, eloquence, and ingenuity. But he is depicted as mischievous, because of his childish tricks—a god with a sense of fun and adventure. There seems something in the character of Hermes that epitomizes space research: the blend of pure science and commercial exploitation; a technology demanding great ingenuity and innovation; yes, and the sense of mischievous adventure that so excites those working in space research but is so loathed by those who believe that the money spent on space should be directed toward more earthly goals. Hermes serves as another symbol for space research, that of messenger. Those who work in the field have a responsibility to get the message of what they are doing, and why, across to the taxpayers who pour billions of dollars into space activities each year. But it isn't just vast amounts of money going into space research; there is also the valuable human resource. Is it surprising that some would ask whether the money and attention would be better directed toward more urgent scientific problems—finding a cure for cancer or the common cold, developing techniques for weather control or for turning desert wasteland into fertile pasture, finding alternative energy sources or substitutes for nonrenewable resources, or whatever.

Humans are curious by nature. It is this curiosity that has set the human species apart from others and enabled us to understand, and to some limited extent to control, our environment. There is no prospect of limiting this curiosity; it knows no bounds. A child is as likely to ask, "How big is the universe?" as to ask, "How does a bird fly?" We are fascinated as much by the distant and unreachable as by things nearby that we can sense by sight, touch, smell, or taste. In studying objects beyond the solar system we may be limited to a single sense, that of sight, but technology has enabled us to extend our vision from gamma rays to radio waves. Science reflects the curiosity of men and women. Curiosity-driven research is an extremely worthwhile activity, to be nurtured and encouraged. We *need* to know more, if the human species is to continue to progress, and if our civilization is to reach its full potential.

Curiosity-based research may be an admirable endeavor. But can we afford to pander to the wishes of a scientific elite spending vast amounts of public money? Here we must make some judgment about the likely long-term value of increased knowledge, plus the potential short-term benefits arising from curiosity-directed research. In the latter, space science scores well. The world has been transformed, one would like to think for the better, by the exploitation of space, in the areas of communications, navigation, weather forecasting, monitoring of the earth's resources, etc. The taxpayers' investment in basic space research (including astronomy from space) has been repaid many times over by the applied technologies that have evolved from it. And we are the richer in knowledge, having learned more about the cosmos in the past few decades than from all previous astronomical research.

But most of space science could (and perhaps should) have been carried out with comparatively cheap unmanned spacecraft. Why the need for expensive, prestigious, high-risk manned missions? Here is where the other objectives for space ventures must be acknowledged—the need to set national goals, the desire to earn international respect through technological achievement, the need to promote science and technology through forefront challenges, the importance of space in global power politics, etc. While not wishing to deny the importance of these objectives, we must admit that they have little to do with science. Yet all too often the blessing of science has been sought by other space objectives in an attempt to legitimize (or disguise) their goals. Thus, for example, although the moon race was born out of Cold War politics, it was justified in the name of science. Yet science alone could never have justified the investment of resources needed for the Apollo program.

It would be wrong to underestimate or dismiss the strategic reasons for being in space. Nor should one berate the adventure element that has inspired brave men and women to explore the uncharted oceans of space. But Hermes must get his message across, clearly and accurately. Science is an enthusiastic user of space, but the cost of space science is a small part of the total space endeavor. People must be fully informed about all the reasons for venturing into space; just one, albeit an important one, being to further basic knowledge. The investment in space science is worthwhile and cost effective; it must fall to others to justify the vast investment in space for adventure, military, commercial, and political ends.

We live in exciting times, especially in science. Few areas of science have generated such excitement as the advances in astronomy, both from the ground and from space. We know more now about the universe than our astronomical forebears could ever have dreamed of, thanks in large part to the achievements from space. But the spectacular advances to date are nothing compared with those expected over the next few decades, so long as our curiosity and excitement for exploring the unknown persist and our commitment to advancement through scientific endeavor is maintained.

One of the great human challenges is to explore the cosmos from space.

POSTSCRIPT
A *Personal View*

I was 13 years old when *Sputnik* was launched. My school headmaster, in my native New Zealand, summoned all his pupils to a special assembly to make the momentous announcement. I can still recall vividly the sense of awe and apprehension that filled me, not helped, I must add, by the headmaster's dire warnings about Soviet might. Yet in the weeks that followed, as I read in scientific magazines about the scientific objectives of the International Geophysical Year (in which *Sputnik*, and the promised U.S. satellites, were meant to play a part), I was confused that wholly admirable scientific objectives (to study the earth's upper atmosphere) were being interpreted by the popular media solely in terms of the Soviet military threat. While much of the global population listened in fear and ignorance to the famous "bleeps" from *Sputnik*, scientists from East and West were using these signals to infer the structure of the upper atmosphere. Later space missions were all too often interpreted in terms of military implications rather than scientific achievement. From its birth, space science was inextricably linked with superpower politics; but today I remain as confused as I was 30 years ago as to why this should necessarily be so.

When I went to university, it was with the initial intention of qualifying to become a telecommunications engineer. But space was now in my blood. I was hooked! Thus when I went on to postgraduate research, I was adamant that my perceived career-training requirements should be matched to my space interests. The connection could, of course, be made via telecommunications satellites. Here was my introduction to the commercial exploitation of space. This is one of the charms of space for scientists—the knowledge that the techniques pioneered by science are so often applicable to projects leading to a better world.

The mid-to-late sixties was a time of unparalleled advances in astronomy. The scientific journals were full of spectacular discoveries of pulsars, quasars, and other exotic phenomena. It seemed to me like a scientific bandwagon that was worth jumping on. So it was farewell, engineering, hello, excitement. And farewell, New Zealand, hello, world. Despite my almost total ignorance of astronomy, my space background seemed sufficient (in the academic climate of the early seventies, distinctly less chilly than today's) to secure me a decade and a half of full-time research in space science and astronomy. I feel enormously privileged to have been able to merge my career and hobby for so long. Fate has been kind to me to have coincided my adult life with the birth of the space age. Despite this general feeling of gratitude, I have long been disturbed that space science, space exploitation, space adventure, and space politics seem hopelessly enmeshed in a web that could yet strangle them all.

Collaboration among scientists can transcend national boundaries in a way possible for few other human activities. International space conferences bring together scientists from East and West, usually with the free exchange of information and ideas. However, such collaborations among individual scientists can often be unworkable because of the paranoia of the space administrators and their political masters. I have encountered this paranoia on numerous occasions. Scientists with common goals who are willing to pursue their research collaboratively are all too often frustrated by political controls. This occurs not just between East and West but also for projects linking allies. Surely scientific collaboration should be a way to build bridges between nations. Yet concerns about technology transfer, unfair commercial advantage, perceived national goals, etc., can sometimes kill the aspirations of scientists at an advanced stage of international collaboration. Sadly, all too often, I have seen agreement reached among scientists of different countries, only to see these agreements overturned by the political juggling of space administrators. The space station was to be a grand Western venture, but has already run afoul of all the usual concerns about technology transfer and security implications. The United States has shown enormous generosity over the decades, opening its space missions to international participation—a generosity certainly never fully matched by its partners. Yet always there is a "them-and-us" stance at the bureaucratic level. If scientists have proved that it is possible to work in genuine collaboration, why does it appear to be so difficult for bureaucrats and politicians?

Space knows no national boundaries. The ocean of space is as truly international as the terrestrial oceans, without the complications of territorial waters. Would it really be outlandish to suggest that space science should be pursued on a genuinely international basis? There have been occasional gestures, such as the joint U.S.-Soviet Apollo-Soyuz mission and U.S. experiments on the *Vega* mission, but mere gestures are all they have really been. (Of course, the collaborations among the Western nations have certainly been more than symbolic gestures.) Need there really have been a moon race twenty years ago? Why are we now embroiled in a space-station showdown? Why do the superpowers find it necessary to stand "eyeball-to-eyeball" on space? Is one really being disloyal to suggest that space should be demilitarized; that ventures such as the space station could be truly international; that Soviets, Europeans, Japanese, and Americans should jointly be planning the return to the moon and the step onward to Mars; that the next generation of space observatories should be planned and exploited by world astronomers regardless of national origin? When I have expounded these views in the past, I have often been told that I am politically naive; my response is always that my accuser is being scientifically shortsighted. If for no other reason than the enormous expense of space endeavors, it must make sense to pursue space-science goals on a genuinely international basis.

The first step toward a global space policy would have to be the genuine demilitarization of space, other than for surveillance—not easy, but surely a laudable goal. Next would need to be an agreement on sharing space technology; this is perhaps even more difficult than the first objective, but can it really be beyond intelligent men and women to reach such an accord? Then fully international agencies covering *all* aspects of space would need to be set up, to agree on long-term international space objectives.

Daydreaming? Perhaps. However, the remarkable achievements in space over a mere three decades almost belie comprehension, and these were mere daydreams during my formative years. Are the political mountains I have defined really any higher than those already conquered by science and engineering? Considering what the "can-do" spirit of scientists and engineers has achieved, perhaps it is now time for the politicians and administrators to set *their* sights on the stars.

INDEX